T2-CSF-302

e hear the voice of God speaking through and apart from those
y with us through life? And how do we find our own voices in
ersations and callings? Leighton Ford's life embodies the good
sus because he is such an extraordinary listener. And through
and articulate remembrance, his story leads us more deeply into

bishop, Florida Conference, the United Methodist Church

s readers deep into his own life, a long journey of listening to the
oice that quietly yet relentlessly called him to his vocations of
t, writer, evangelist, and mentor. A master stylist, he nudges
o a rushing stream of arresting verbs, memorable phrases, and
tories of loss and redemption. With this book, Ford gives the
oir new and unforgettable meaning."

ker, author of *One Soul at a Time: The Story of Billy Graham*

n grateful for the voice of Leighton Ford in my life for the past
rs. The person who has 'ears to hear' and a willingness to listen
he voice of the Lord in these deep and insightful pages from his
inistry."

h, archbishop, Anglican Church in North America

eople talk about hearing God, but Leighton Ford embodies this
pouring his wisdom and life experiences into these pages, Ford
ur spiritual director, walking with us as we walk with God. A
for anyone who strives to cling more closely to the Savior!"

ssie Martin, assistant professor of ministry and leadership development,
nwell Theological Seminary

e twenty years I have *listened* to the life of Leighton Ford through
lling, art, preaching, and mentoring and walking with me. I have
my own call through his *listening* to me. Like his life, this book
ep wisdom to people who are thirsty to hear and know God in an
listening is rare. Read and listen."

Morse, professor, author, and friend

"Leighton Ford's *A Life of Listening* is a
from years of ministry, encouraging us to
tions. As we read of his experiences and ir
history of ministry, watch for his mentor
calls us to be attentive to voices of the Spir
Brian C. Stiller, Global Ambassador, The Wo

"Leighton Ford has been a giant in the ev
a century. In this memoir we hear of the
his gentle, wise, and kind voice. Reading
luminous presence, emerging with a voice
strangely, more profoundly our own."
Jason Byassee, Butler Chair in Homiletics and
Vancouver School of Theology, author of *Surpr*

"Reading Leighton Ford's remarkable story
more attentively to God's voice in my stor
Steve A. Brown, president, Arrow Leadership,
Practices for a Christian Leader's Most Important

"*A Life of Listening* is a jewel. Leighton For
saint who has learned to listen to the livin;
to sit at his feet reading this book, as he sha
with vulnerability and with the authorit
Shepherd's voice."
Sarah Breuel, Revive Europe director, evangeli
International Fellowship of Evangelical Studen

"You may never have the opportunity to s
Leighton share stories of hope, heartache, c
but I invite you to listen through this bool
who has been refined beautifully through t
throughout the Lausanne Movement that I
Michael Oh, global executive director/chief exe

"This book is a rich commentary on the prov
story is woven into each of our stories in ways
Don't miss reading this—as you are likely to
Jim Singleton, associate professor of pastoral le
Gordon-Conwell Theological Seminary

"How do
who jou
these co
news of
vulnerab
our own
Ken Cart

"Ford dra
one true
poet, ar
readers
gripping
genre *m*
Grant W

"I have b
twenty y
will hea
life and
Foley Be

"So man
reality.
become
must-re
Nicole M
Gordon-

"Over so
his story
discover
speaks
age whe
MaryKa

"Behold,
I stand at
the door…"
Jesus, Revelation 3:20

Mr Jimmy R Butler
1357 Blossom Hill Way
Roseville, CA 95661

Lib
R 10/12/21

A LIFE OF
LISTENING

DISCERNING
GOD'S VOICE
AND
DISCOVERING
OUR OWN

A MEMOIR BY

LEIGHTON FORD

An imprint of InterVarsity Press
Downers Grove, Illinois

InterVarsity Press
P.O. Box 1400, Downers Grove, IL 60515-1426
ivpress.com
email@ivpress.com

©2019 by Leighton Ford

All rights reserved. No part of this book may be reproduced in any form without written permission from InterVarsity Press.

InterVarsity Press® is the book-publishing division of InterVarsity Christian Fellowship/USA®, a movement of students and faculty active on campus at hundreds of universities, colleges, and schools of nursing in the United States of America, and a member movement of the International Fellowship of Evangelical Students. For information about local and regional activities, visit intervarsity.org.

All Scripture quotations, unless otherwise indicated, are taken from The Holy Bible, New International Version®, NIV®. Copyright © 1973, 1978, 1984, 2011 by Biblica, Inc.™ Used by permission of Zondervan. All rights reserved worldwide. www.zondervan.com. The "NIV" and "New International Version" are trademarks registered in the United States Patent and Trademark Office by Biblica, Inc.™

While any stories in this book are true, some names and identifying information may have been changed to protect the privacy of individuals.

Cover design: Cindy Kiple
Interior design: Daniel van Loon
Images: © Drunaa / Trevillion Images

ISBN 978-0-8308-4573-6 (print)
ISBN 978-0-8308-5799-9 (digital)

Printed in the United States of America ∞

InterVarsity Press is committed to ecological stewardship and to the conservation of natural resources in all our operations. This book was printed using sustainably sourced paper.

Library of Congress Cataloging-in-Publication Data
A catalog record for this book is available from the Library of Congress.

P 25 24 23 22 21 20 19 18 17 16 15 14 13 12 11 10 9 8 7 6 5 4 3 2 1

Y 37 36 35 34 33 32 31 30 29 28 27 26 25 24 23 22 21 20 19

To those younger (or once younger)

kingdom-seekers, friends on the journey,

who have listened patiently to my stories

and shared their own

And to our beloved grandchildren,

Graham, Christine and Ben, Anabel and Leighton,

who I pray will carry the Jesus story on

Then pay attention to how you listen.

LUKE 8:18 NRSV

CONTENTS

INTRODUCTION

A Testament of Listening

*"Faith comes from hearing, and hearing
through the word of Christ."*

Romans 10:17 ESV

Not long ago I took our daughter Debbie and two of our
grown grandchildren on a memory trip to places in Canada
where I grew up.

One special spot we visited was on Lake Rosseau in the
Muskoka lakes region. It was once the site of a Bible conference,
long since defunct, where my mother took me many summers of
my early life.

As we cruised by boat along the rocky shore, I could see the old
buildings derelict and deserted, but the memories stayed with me.
I recalled the children's meetings where a retired missionary
woman and a college student told us about Jesus, and how at the

end of that week I put up my hand to say I wanted to know and follow him.

The leaders said I was too young. But after I lifted my hand three times they realized I knew what I wanted, at least as much as a child could take in.

I was five then. Now, eighty plus years later, I can barely recall the voices and faces of that missionary lady and that college student, but I know that through them I heard another Voice calling me, a voice I have been listening for ever since. So I write my listening story not because it is a perfect story or one to emulate but as a testament to the power of listening for the voice of my Lord.

Did I always listen to what the poet Mary Oliver called his "incomparably lovely young-man voice"? No, not always. Often I have been too busy, too preoccupied with my own thoughts, too intent on having my own way or waywardness. Yet often, when I have truly listened, that other Voice has spoken quietly but insistently.

Did I sometimes mistake my own voice for that Other? No doubt, but when I have stopped to pay attention I have recognized, through and beyond my own and other voices, the Voice of One who speaks with accents of truth, love, beauty, and grace.

I truly believe—from the Holy Scriptures and my own experience—that out of the many voices that speak to us, voices of blessing or otherwise, as we discern the Voice of the Great Shepherd, we find our own deepest identity.

As that splendid poet Gerard Manley Hopkins wrote, each mortal thing cries, "What I do is me, for that I came." Then in a magnificent image he writes that "Christ plays in ten thousand places, lovely in limbs and lovely in eyes not his, to the Father, through the features of men's faces."

Hopkins's words resonate with the biblical promise that we can be changed, transformed. They are also in sync with neuro-scientists who study the brain, who are telling us that our brains are not totally hardwired, that they can be rewired.

So I truly believe, as we listen deeply and faithfully to Christ the Living Word, as his words in Scripture and his Spirit indwell our brains and imaginations, we may discern *his* voice through *ten thousand voices*, and heeding, become the persons we were created to be and long to be.

I hope you may find my story interesting and encouraging. But more than that, I pray it will be to you an invitation not just to listen on occasion but to *be a listener*, one who pays attention to the God who speaks.

THE EARLIEST VOICES

For you have been my hope, Sovereign LORD,
my confidence since my youth.

PSALM 71:5

No matter how hard I try, I cannot remember the sound of my mother's voice.

I can summon to mind her appearance—short and stern, fashionably dressed. But when I try to recall the tone, the scale, the rhythm of her speech, some inflection—nothing comes. Others tell me she sounded like an old-time schoolmarm, her voice high-pitched and thin like a bird's.

Maybe it's because she was my adoptive mother, not my birth mother. But I did not know that for the first dozen years of my life.

Or maybe it's because while I was growing up, my mother would spend hours lecturing me—her preferred method of correction. So I may have blocked it out. It was as if hers was a voice that I heard, and heard, and heard, and then had to stop hearing.

There is another Voice who has been calling to me all my life, like somebody I already know, somebody I know I will recognize on meeting for the first time. It is the invisible thread twining through my life, drawing all other threads together. When I finally meet this Voice, I will be face-to-face with Jesus. He will speak my true name. I will answer and for the first time hear the sound of my own true voice. I will know that, finally, I have come all the way home.

This invisible thread began its weaving through my life long before I was aware of it. My mother's was the first voice that spoke to me, earliest and most insistently. In those years the Voice sounded very like my mother. It took me a long time to tell the difference.

I was born with long legs and given a long name—the long legs from my biological father, the names from my adoptive mother, Olive.

I found out I was adopted on an autumn afternoon when my mother took me for a walk in Toronto's High Park. She had a purpose for that walk, as she did for most things. She had decided it was time to tell me a secret held from me all these years—that I was adopted.

"There was an accident," she told me, explaining about my birth parents. For a long time I assumed they must have been killed in a car wreck. It was years before I realized I was the "accident."

"We didn't have to adopt you," she said as we walked among the rough russet maple leaves. "We chose you. And we love you."

Why did she wait that long? I have no idea. I must have been very naive or I would have guessed it long before, because by this time I was over six feet tall and my mother barely four foot eleven and my father also short. Clearly, we had different genes!

I did not feel troubled about the adoption. Rather, being chosen made me feel special and later also gave me a sense of how significant it is when the Bible says God "adopts" us into his family.

Soon after I was born, my adopted parents, Charles and Olive Ford, took me to Chatham, Ontario—the "Maple City" in southern Ontario known for the magnificent trees that burst into color every fall—where they ran a jewelry store.

It was about as British a provincial Canadian city as it could be: Chatham in Kent County with the Thames River running through it, replicating the old country. The first settlers clearly wanted to keep their loyalty to king and crown. The street names were very English—King Street, where Ford's Jewelers was located, and Victoria Avenue, where our first home stood.

These English-sounding streets and river were intersected by Tecumseh Park, named after the famed Indian chief killed in battle a few miles upriver at Moraviantown. There was also a small population known as "colored" people in Chatham and district, descendants of former slaves who escaped from the United States to new homes in Canada via the Underground Railway. One terminal of their route was only two or three blocks from our store.

Our small city was a market center for the farmers. Many of them were Dutch immigrants, who grew their sugar beets and tobacco on the rich lands around the city and came to town on a Saturday night to shop and drink good, dark Dutch beer, hopefully spending some of their hard-earned money at our store.

Although my parents had lost most of their savings and investments during the Great Depression, business was steady. My father was the watchmaker, my mother the buyer with a good eye for fashion. Yet she was always worried about not having enough money.

But there was enough for her to buy fine clothes, and she took frequent buying trips to Detroit, an hour away. Sometimes she took along a retired Salvation Army woman officer, Major Lindsay, thinking the customs officers at the border—seeing her religious uniform—would not ask too many questions about what Mom had bought when they came back to Canada.

After school I often did my homework at the store, where Mom and Dad both worked, sometimes playing games of hide-and-seek with a friend in the long basement storage room or in the underground halls of the hotel building where they rented space. When I was older I also helped with sales during busy times.

One night during Christmas rush when they were both at work, I remember feeling a terrible fear of being left alone. I was an only child, although two or three foster girls lived with us at times. On this night I was there by myself, both my mother and father working late. I woke in a panic when I realized no one else was in the house and was so frightened that I called a taxi and had the driver take me to the store, still dressed in my pajamas.

I wonder if all adopted children have native loneliness embedded deep in the psyche, a subconscious fear of being abandoned that can be triggered anytime.

——◊——

I had friends enough in those younger years, but as far I can remember my parents had few. I can't recollect them ever entertaining for a meal or a party, nor did we eat together at home very often. Except for breakfast, most of our meals—of mine—for years were taken at one of the hotel restaurants along King Street or at Rexall Drugs, where I loved a grilled cheese sandwich and coke for lunch.

On our dining room wall is my painting of the house where I lived as a boy at 283 Victoria Avenue, a fine two-story wooden house with white walls and blue trim. It is a late-afternoon scene, and the long shadows of the evergreens fall across the lawn toward the house. In the foreground are the brilliant branches of a maple tree in full autumn glory. A set of windows on the side takes me back years, three multipaned dormer windows jutting out from a sitting room. Just inside was an alcove with a brown cabinet radio, where in the late afternoons I listened to radio serials—The Lone Ranger; Jack Armstrong, the All-American Boy; The Green Hornet. On Saturday nights in winter I sat glued to the radio listening to Foster Hewitt announce, "From downtown Toronto's Maple Leaf Gardens, it's hockey night in Canada," and dreamed that someday I too would be a hockey broadcaster.

I loved sports. But as a boy I was too shy and gangly to be good at them. Later I found I had a strong competitive streak and quick reflexes, enough to play goalie in hockey and later to slam returns at the net in tennis. But in the early years my mother, always protective, never encouraged me in sports. She had a different interest to instill in me.

For Mother the choice to adopt was made not only out of love but for what she believed was a God-given purpose. When I was a few days old, she took me to be dedicated to the Lord by Dr. Henry Frost, a missionary leader. He said, "Mrs. Ford, I believe God has given you this child for a purpose," and she often reminded me of what he said.

Mother held onto that purpose. She had wanted to be a missionary. As a child she sang "I'm going to the Congo, the call is growing stronger . . ." The call may have seemed strong, but she was not fit to be a missionary. So, her own dream unfulfilled, she looked for a child to adopt to live out that calling.

The adoption was privately arranged after she had picked me and checked out my birth parents. Her son needed the right blood lines to fulfill the purpose she (and presumably God) had for him—for me.

She also was the one who named me—Leighton Frederick Sandys Ford—each name carrying a special meaning for her. "Leighton" was after the first Canadian ambassador to the United States, Leighton McCarthy. "Frederick" was from the uncle she adored who left his studies for the Anglican ministry to enlist in the Canadian army and was killed at the Battle of Vimy Ridge in France during the Great War. "Sandys" was after an Anglican deaconess from an aristocratic family in our city, whom she greatly admired. Those names, in almost a biblical sense, signified to her my calling, and hers.

She was a small but very determined woman who compensated for her stature by identifying with Queen Victoria (who was also quite short) by wearing lifts in her shoes to add an inch or so of height. She prided herself on being an astute business woman, the brains behind the business, with a special knack of choosing the fine jewelry for their store. She dressed quite fashionably in her fur coats and feathered hats in winter and summer frocks.

—◦◦◦—

My earliest image of coming before God is of myself as a small boy, kneeling at a prayer bench on the second floor of that frame house on Victoria Avenue. It consisted of a kind of wooden prie-dieu with a slanted top and shelves, and a small stool, placed in an alcove against the railing at the top of our stairs.

There, day after day, and what seemed sometimes hour after hour, Mother would have me kneel to memorize Bible verses. I would dutifully repeat prayers after her word by word, all the while hoping I could soon escape and go out to play.

Why that didn't turn me off to prayer forever I am not sure, except that I was a dutiful child, and she was determined to shape me for what she was sure was my calling. As she would often remind me, holding up books about famous missionaries and preachers, "Leighton, God is looking for more men like this." It was clear in her mind—and I suppose in mine—that I was to be one of them.

Those sessions seemed endless, and my mind wandered outside where I wanted to be playing with my friends. But they did imprint on my mind that life had a great purpose, that the world was bigger than our small city, and that I was to be part of that purpose and that world.

My mother reinforced that purpose in every way she could, making sure there was a spiritual input to every activity.

She and I often took the train to Toronto for her to shop for fine clothes. On these trips my only escape from boredom was reading. I was allowed to purchase the latest edition of *Chums: The Boys' Own Annual*, and I could lose myself in the adventure stories of explorers while she had her hair done. On one of these trips we went to a large church to hear a visiting preacher, who had been chief of chaplains in the British army. "Listen," she whispered, poking me in the side, "That is a very great man. God wants more like him."

Voices by the Lake

In Chatham she felt smothered and deprived of strong Bible teaching. So from the time I was five she took me each summer to the Canadian Keswick Conference, a spiritual center in the Muskoka Lakes of Ontario. Most vacationers went for fun, food, water sports. Devout Christians went there for rest and spiritual renewal.

For a young lad the trip itself was an adventure. A three-and-a-half-hour train ride on the Canadian National or Canadian Pacific railroads to Toronto. A change of trains at the cavernous Union Station. Then the exciting two-plus hours north to the lake country.

My mother saw to it that my Bible learning began as we traveled. Once on the train she made me memorize Jesus' long prayer in the seventeenth chapter of John's Gospel. I can still repeat his words from the old King James: "These words spake Jesus, and lifted up his eyes to heaven, and said . . ."

Once in Muskoka we would catch a lake steamer to the village of Port Carling. There we switched to take the *Ahmic* through the twisting Indian River to Keswick. Captain Hill, who commanded the ship, was fascinating to me, both because he was missing a thumb and because sometimes he would let me come into the cabin and steer as he directed me through the straits—telling me to move the wheel "one spoke to the left, two to the right."

Keswick was set in a cove, snuggled under some hills, and full of the scent of summer firs. There was one hill especially that I loved to climb by myself when I was old enough. At the top was a rocky place with a view of the lake and beyond. Our own hometown was in the flat, sugar-beet farmlands of southwestern Ontario, a fertile but not a very inspiring landscape. In contrast the loveliness of the hills and rocks and lakes of Muskoka infused into my soul a love for high places and water, which remains to this day.

After the first summer or two my mother arranged for us to stay for a month in a canvas cabin on a rocky knoll where a wooden platform formed the base for this cabin, pieces of canvas squares on wooden frames. From there we set out each morning for the daily Bible lectures in the eight-sided Delectable Mansion. For me the serious side was more than offset by the fun events— tennis, lawn bowling and croquet, pickup softball games with the staff (most of whom were Bible college students), and afternoon swims in the cove.

Many sounds come back to me, many voices from those summer days.

The most lasting were from what was called the "Galilee Cathedral," a kind of outdoor chapel built into a slope down to the water and named for the lake where Jesus called his disciples and taught the crowds. After supper most nights, a missionary hour took place in this outdoor sanctuary.

Rows of steps were shaped leading down to the lakeside. On each were wooden benches, supports and backs and arm rests still rough with bark. A small platform made with native Muskoka stone jutted out into the lake, and standing on it one or more missionaries would tell their stories. Some were attractive, full of life and wonderful accounts. Some droned on. Two voices from that lakeside remain with me. There were the voices telling of faraway places—Ethiopia, the Solomon Islands, China, the heart of Africa. From them I learned that Mussolini's Italian army had invaded Ethiopia, land of the "Lion of Judah," the emperor Haile Selassie. These voices made me conscious of the vast world beyond my own small Ontario town and began to form in me a world consciousness.

Then there was the voice of the lake itself, the gentle waters of Lake Rosseau lapping up on the shore as we sang and the missionaries spoke. It was a lulling, almost hypnotizing voice. Quiet as these waves were, they must have drowned out the painful efforts of some of the less inspirational missionaries. The waves were the voice of calm. Even as I remember them now I want to go and sit there, let hours pass beyond "the hour," and allow the peace that seldom was found in our home to settle into my spirit.

When the time came to leave, the lake steamer would come to pick up departing guests. Everyone would trek down to the pier for goodbyes led by Rowland Bingham, the *éminence gris* of Keswick. A small man with a long rather dog-like face who always wore a multicolored pin-striped blazer, he was remarkable, with vision far beyond his size, a founder of the Sudan Interior Mission, and a man whose faith and prayers infused the spirit of Keswick.

As the ship left he would wave his hands and start us singing Keswick's traditional farewell song:

Faith, mighty faith, the promise sees,
and looks to God alone,
laughs at impossibilities,
and cries it shall be done.[1]

The ship would chug away. Keswick's rocky point would disappear around a bend.

We would be off from delectable mansions to a world of war, of foreign missions, of ordinary school days in unglamorous homes and towns, but with a sense that we had been in touch for a few days or weeks with something beyond the humdrum of daily life.

Voices from the world. The voice of the lake. They were forming in me, unconsciously, the twin longings of my soul: to go and simply to be.

On the return train ride to Toronto we would pass through the small city of Orillia, set by another lake, Lake Simcoe.

There, nearly half a century later, I would meet another mother, the one who gave me birth, who also listened to her own voices by the lake, some with a very different tone.

But for now, Olive was the first "voice" of my calling. Through her efforts I was surrounded by God's voice, and yet it was also a voice that sounded at times like her own. I understood very little then of the demons that drove her from which I would need to be free.

Sifting

I have known since my earliest years that God was calling to me, that he knew my name(s) better than I did. But in later years I have found myself sifting through all the voices that have called my name, contemplating the different ways in which I have heard God's voice speaking through them. As you read my story, perhaps it will stir a remembering of the voices you have heard in your life—those you have been guided by, those you might have forgotten, those you long to hear once again.

Together, let's listen for the Voice of our calling—the sound of God at work in our lives, weaving all things together in a tapestry of divine artistry. When we walk in the light, as God is in the light, we become fellow travelers on the path that leads through dark places as well as bright. In the words of Leonard Cohen:

Ring the bells that still can ring
Forget your perfect offering
There is a crack in everything
That's how the light gets in[2]

And, I would add, that's how the light gets out.

❧ 2 ❧

DISCERNING ONE VOICE
FROM ANOTHER

Give your servant a discerning heart.

1 KINGS 3:9

In a dream, I am a young boy in my parents' store doing my homework on the small mezzanine.

I hear children's voices at play in the nearby park and run out to join them. As I leave I glance down the street, and there at the corner is my mother in her feathered hat, waiting for the light to turn. She gives a knowing smile—like "gotcha"—and raises her hands, huge in the dream, as if to say "stop." I do. I stop. I run back into the store.

Those hands must have stayed in my subconscious for years, telling me to stay where I was supposed to, reminding me that we, my mother and I, were to be different, "better than" others.

That dream made me realize how much of my life was driven by a voice that kept asking, Am I measuring up? When I missed one word in a spelling contest at school, I left the room in tears. In most everything—studies, sports, preaching, writing, leadership, painting—I felt I had to measure up.

I heard the devout voice of my adoptive mother, Olive, early on. But there was another voice. A disturbed one.

Her high dreams were haunted by deep fears, mostly about money. My father had invested in stocks purchased on the margin, most lost in the stock market crash of the early 1930s. As the years passed, Mom became convinced that he was living a deceptive life, had other women, and was gambling away her share of the business profits.

She feared he was conspiring to have her put away in an institution for the mentally ill. I had no reason to believe her suspicions had any grounds, but I was too naive then to realize she was ill, afflicted with a classic case of paranoia.

Although I cannot recall her ordinary voice, I can remember hearing her shrieking more than once. The house bordering Tecumseh Park, where we had moved during my high school years, became a battleground at night when I would wake to hear her screaming, accusing Dad of hiding money. He would barricade his bedroom door with a dresser or lock himself in the bathroom and flush the toilet over and over to drown the sound, while I buried my fourteen-year-old head under a pillow.

A Bleak Winter

The winter of 1945-1946 was a bleak one for me. World War II had ended the previous summer. The initial celebrations had faded, leaving exhaustion behind. On Christmas Day of 1945 we had lunch, then went to see the movie *Leave Her to Heaven*—a lurid drama about a long-suffering husband and his homicidally jealous wife. Afterward, we went back to the store to clean up some post-holiday business.

Mother had begun to badger Dad while he busied himself at his watchmaker's bench, trying to ignore her. One time, still wearing her hat and winter coat, she grabbed the top of a large black safe and hung there, kicking her legs and shrieking in fury. I stood watching, behind the large counter that ran the length of the store, frightened and helpless.

At the end of the Christmas season the war between my parents exploded, leading to my mother's abrupt disappearance a few days later. I had no idea where she had gone. I was left largely alone in our blue stucco house, going back and forth to school and store and home, wondering at her absence but relieved the fighting was past. It was a small city, and I'm sure there were employees at the store and neighbors who gossiped about her absence, but nobody mentioned it to me. I kept busy with my studies at the Chatham Collegiate, taking eight or nine demanding courses. At night I was virtually alone except for Alden, a girl my parents had employed to help with chores at home and the store. Dad was gone almost every night working.

Much later I learned that Mother had gone nearly a thousand miles away to Winnipeg, living in disguise under an assumed name, trying to foil Dad's supposed plan to have her committed for treatment.

Somehow those months passed, and in late spring she returned, and we resumed our "normal" life together.

Learning to Discern

Wading in the memories of those early waters, what do I sense now toward Olive? In many ways she is to me more like a character in a novel than a real person. So many years have passed. So many conflicting experiences color my memory of her.

What would it be like if I could sit down to talk with her now when I am older than she was when she died? I think I would have a mixture of foreboding, gratitude, pity, anger, relief.

There might be a knot in my stomach, fearing it would lead to one of those interminable one-way lectures.

Gratitude that I was chosen, loved, provided for.

Pity for the fears which cobbled her.

Anger for the way she treated my father and tried not to let me go.

Relief that I was able to find true freedom in who Christ has called me to be.

Other voices had been opening up my life in new ways. So, I could also say to my mother, "Thanks for taking me where I would hear about Jesus and learn about God's Word. For holding before me the ideal of serving the Lord. For helping me to know that the world was a much bigger place than our little corner of Canada. For seeing that I had a capacity for deep feeling and imagination—a poetic voice as it were, even though it has taken me time to find it."

What I might not tell her is that, unwittingly, she also gave me a negative gift of discernment. I learned that not everything she said God wanted for me was God's idea. I had to sort out what were merely her desires.

Because of this came a sense of shrewdness about those who claim they have a word from God for us, an understanding that a "testing of the spirits" must be practiced.

In those years I was learning that the "incomparable voice" of the Lord may come through voices that contain seeds of truth but also carry distorted messages. Discerning God's true call both *through* and *apart from* them is a large part of spiritual maturing.

Gordon Smith's counsel is helpful:

No one can presume to discern for another. . . .

This is why discernment is such a vital skill in the Christian life. We can discern only for ourselves. Further, we mature in the Christian faith only when we learn to discern for ourselves and thus develop the capacity, and hopefully the courage, to listen and act in a manner congruent with the voice of Jesus.[1]

How do we discern God's voice, whether through or apart from our parents? This is for most of us a lifelong quest, our parents' voices echoing in our memories way past childhood.

As a small child I needed to honor and obey my mother. Even though I often turned my mind elsewhere when sitting through her interminable lectures, I learned from her.

As I grew older I needed to learn to think my own thoughts, trust my own heart, and measure what she said against what I sensed to be God's will.

I do think her voice was used to let me know there was a big world out there and that I was called to play my own singular part in God's redeeming will for the world. By exposing me to the Bible and the example of others, she was, without realizing it, allowing me to listen beyond her voice to other voices.

Although back then I couldn't have described what was happening, I was beginning to test my decision-making and find my voice.

I was beginning to listen for that other Voice, remembering that at a wedding Mary had said, "Do whatever he tells you" (John 2:5).

I would like to think, wistfully, that in a different time, that was also what my mother, Olive, might have said.

—◦◦◦—

If there'd been a barometer in our house that registered emotional pressure, more often than not it would have read "stormy."

My father and mother had started in the jewelry trade business in Deseronto, Ontario, then bought a store in Chatham. But they were far from partners in marriage, which is one of the reasons my father spent most of his time at the store.

The four blocks of King Street in Chatham were lined with small businesses. My parents' store was on the high-value block in the William Pitt Hotel building, squeezed in between Laura Secord Candies and a men's clothing shop.

One of the few photos I have of my father (from the late 1920s or early 1930s) shows him behind the counter of this long and narrow store. It has no modern lines with curves and open spaces. It has an old-fashioned box shape, with high and horizontal lines of windows and shelves, a long carpeted floor, a vertical radiator, and hanging lights.

The display cases are jammed with goods. Costume jewelry, watches, and fine rings stretch two-thirds of the way in showcases on the left side. Shelves of silverware line the wall behind; a single shelf on the right side holds wooden clocks. A set of stairs leads up to a half mezzanine, set off by a wooden railing. A large safe divides the sales area from the workbenches at the rear.

My father stands behind the counter, hands in the pockets of a tweed-looking jacket and dark tie. He has a neat moustache. A lock of his dark hair falls across the right side of his forehead.

In this photo, likely taken in his thirties, he looks rather trim. I remember him later as of medium height and build, about 5'6", a bit portly, usually wearing a long-sleeved shirt and tie. The moustache disappeared across the years. That bit of hair kept straying across his forehead.

The sign on the front window said, "Charles R. Ford, Jeweler." It was my mother, Olive, though, who so often claimed she was the "brains behind the business." She was a good businesswoman who did most of the buying and had an eye for what would sell.

If she was the brains, Dad was the "hands" that made it go. He was a skilled watchmaker who learned his trade from his uncle's store in Hamilton, Ontario.

I picture him bent over his workbench, eyeglass in place as he peers and pokes at the inside of a watch. Sometimes he straightens to puff on a cigar or the pipe that was perpetually beside him. Or I can see him at the counter, chatting up a customer who comes in to talk. He was the proverbial "hail-fellow-well-met." His demeanor was diffident. His voice was friendly and quiet, except for the times he yelled in fury at Mom in one of their frequent spats.

Did she ever give him a compliment? I can't remember. As for her beliefs that he was gambling, drinking, and wasting their money on other women, I may have been naive, but I never saw any of that, although I am sure he had the occasional beer.

He may not have been totally browbeaten but certainly was much berated. When she was most bitter about their marriage, she would resort to quoting a strange saying: "The lowest man in England is the lowest man's wife."

How did he survive their years together? It is a mystery to me. I often wonder how they ever came to be married, although there was at times a little tender affection between them, but that was rare. Storms were always in the air.

Dad was seldom at home except to sleep, and that was often interrupted by her middle-of-the-night tirades. He spent most of his time in the store, all day and usually after supper. It was more his home than our houses ever were.

His one recreation was lawn bowling. I would stand at the fence and watch him send his much admired fast bowl to scatter the balls at the far end. He took me a few times to watch Gordie Howe play for the Detroit Red Wings and to Tigers baseball games at Briggs Stadium.

He was not a church-going man, although he had been an altar boy in a high Anglican Church. I cannot remember him ever going to church with us—unless for some patriotic occasion. Mom's hyperspirituality linked with her sharp tongue and disdain must have turned him off.

He was generous with me and my friends. One friend remembers that we wanted to go to Detroit for a weekend to attend a youth rally. My friend's parents didn't have money for those trips, so my dad doled out the cash for both of us.

What touched Dad's heart was the singing of George Beverly Shea, the soloist on *Songs in the Night*, broadcast late Sunday evenings from Chicago. Dad would sit in our living room and listen to Bev's deep voice, tears streaming down his face.

3

CHOOSING TO BECOME
A LISTENER

Speak, for your servant is listening.

1 Samuel 3:10

That year when my mother left us could have been a terribly lonely time as I finished my first year of high school. But I had friends, especially Danny Goldsmith, whom I had known since fifth grade when we traded postage stamps. Danny and I would walk home from high school together. Sometimes I'd play the piano, and we would sing some of the pop tunes of the day. Other times we'd play rugby at Tecumseh Park. Once I even persuaded my dad to buy me a pair of skis. That was weird because there were no hills for miles around except for a tiny twenty-foot slope on the riverbank of the park. Our attempts were a total mess up, and Danny nearly ended up in the river.

In late spring or summer Mother returned from her strange self-induced exile, and things returned to what passed as normal.

She became interested in a new Bible conference called Blue Water, located on a riverside a few miles away. Except for the vivid blue river, the Bible conference grounds were unimpressive, nothing to equal the beauty of the lakes and rocks in the Muskoka region. But it did promise a change in the middle of a boring summer. Mother signed me up, and Danny and I went together.

I went dutifully to the Bible teaching sessions in a plain cinderblock building, expecting to be bored, but it turned out to be more interesting than I expected. I liked the other young people, especially a cute hostess who caught my eye, although I was too shy even to say hello to her. I liked the way the other attendees prayed spontaneously and the gospel choruses they sang, which were new to me.

The featured teacher that week was Oswald Smith, well known as the pastor of a large church. For some reason he had agreed to spend a week at this obscure, nondescript fledgling place. I remember he had silvery gray hair swept back, startlingly blue eyes, and a voice that was gravelly and piercing. He announced his text: "Psalm five verse three. The only verse in the Bible that speaks twice of morning."

I thumbed through a Thompson Chain Reference Bible my mother had given me for my fourteenth birthday and located the text (which I still have underlined in that Bible): "My voice shalt thou hear in the morning, O Lord; in the morning will I direct my prayer unto thee, and will look up" (Psalm 5:3 KJV).

"My topic is the Morning Watch," he said.

I slumped back. What teenager wanted to watch anything in the morning? But when he began to tell us *how* he prayed, I sat up.

"I am a very nervous person," he told us. "I find it hard to sit still. So when I pray I don't kneel down, I don't sit down, I don't stand. I walk up and down."

That was a new idea: I could pray and exercise at the same time.

"I have a very busy mind," he went on. "I get easily distracted. So I pray out loud instead of just thinking my prayers. So I don't keep using the same words over and over, I read a verse, perhaps from the psalms, and turn that into a prayer."

That stirred my imagination. I sensed a strong urge to pray in a whole new way, not with rote words my mother had me repeat but in my own heart language. And I decided to try.

Early the next morning I walked out to a grove of woods and rambled among the trees, Bible in hand, a bit embarrassed, hoping no one would see me. I opened to one of the psalms and read it out loud, making it a prayer.

What those verses were I have no idea, but I must have prayed something like this: "God, you search me. You know me. How lonely I have been with Mom gone. She and Dad fighting so much of the time. I need you to be with me. Please be real to me, as you are to the other young people here. Help me to look up to you in the morning, as Dr. Smith said last night. Thank you that you care and understand. And show me what you want me to do."

Did I sense God speaking back to me that morning? I think so, at least inwardly. I do know that I had a new and deeper understanding of how personally God cared for this teenage boy. A small flame began to burn in my heart.

Listening with a Difference

On a morning sixty-plus years later, I drove with some friends twenty miles west of Chatham to find the site of Blue Water. Everything was so changed that I could not remember the way. I spotted a farm supply store and asked the owner if he remembered what used to be a conference center.

"Oh," he said, "you mean the Blue Water place. It ran down and then burned down, and they closed it years back. But some weird group took it over." He pointed down a side road and told us to look for a sign.

We made our way along the road running by bright blue water until we spotted the sign. A driveway led through a grassy field to a large house made of sections stuck together, surrounded by a collection of old trailers and derelict blackened cabins, a straggly row of trees, some unkempt lawns. Blue Water seemed a very plain and sparse place.

An elderly woman cleaning out a trailer said this indeed was the Blue Water site before it shut down. She and her husband still led prayer groups. "Once we prayed so hard the fire of the Lord fell," she reminisced. "The word got around there was a fire, and the local fire trucks came to put it out!"

It was hard for me to imagine there had ever been a spiritual conflagration in this derelict place, but I remembered what had fired my heart.

I tried to retrace my long ago prayer path to a small copse of trees where I went by myself to pray. The grove seemed much smaller.

What, I wondered, had left its mark on me long ago? Why here and why then?

I suppose I became a listener, or, as author Basil Pennington puts it, "a listening." It was not just the act of hearing a preacher that night but the reality of becoming a listener. Before I *had* to listen to Mom's voice. I now *chose* to be a listener for God's voice for myself.

Listening in an Ordinary Place

Why did it happen at this ramshackle place, with only the vivid blue of the water as a hint of beauty? Perhaps the very ordinariness of the place led to an out-of-ordinary encounter. It has happened before in holy history.

Jacob, fleeing from his revenge-seeking brother, Esau, whom he had cheated out of his birthright, slept in the solitary desert with his head on a rock. That night he had a memorable dream of a ladder with angels ascending and descending. In the morning he woke with a startling certainty: "Surely the LORD is in this place, and I was not aware of it."

"How awesome is *this place!*" Jacob exclaimed. "This is none other than the house of God; this is the gate of heaven" (Genesis 28:16-17). And he named the place Bethel.

Was the desert any different the morning after his dream? His stone pillow was still rock hard. The sands of the desert were dry and scorching. The landscape stretched across barren paths. But while the landscape was the same, his inscape was changed. To the eyes of his soul, this had become a "thin place," as the ancient Celts would have described it. It was made so not by any beauty but by the promise of a Presence in an ordinary place.

And why for me, then, that summer when I was fourteen? Adolescence is typically the time when conversions (of various types) take place. This was not exactly a conversion for me, but it was a very special awakening.

Was it perhaps the voice of *difference*? A different setting?

Or was it the voice of *absence*? Samuel's mother Hannah took him to the temple and left him there to serve God with the priest Eli. There he too became a listener. Three times he heard his name called, "Samuel, Samuel." Three times he went to Eli asking if he had called. Then the old priest helped him to distinguish God's voice in his soul from Eli's voice in his ear. And so he prayed, "Speak, for your servant is listening" (1 Samuel 3:10).

Was it for me also the voice of *separation*? Of a new self-differentiation and God awareness? For Augustine, a journey from his mother, Monica, in North Africa to distant Rome brought him to a moment in the garden, when he heard a voice that forever changed him: "Take and read."

Was it perhaps the voice of *loneliness*? Of a teenager who had spent those nights listening to arguing voices? Or those long months alone when my mother was gone?

Was it, perhaps most of all, the voice of *longing*, longing for the reality of God? Perhaps that drab and flat piece of ground, framing the most vivid blue water I had ever seen, created the hunger for the beauty of the Lord in the dry ground of life.

Perhaps the psalm I prayed in that morning prayer walk included this:

You, God, are my God,
> earnestly I seek you;
I thirst for you,
> my whole being longs for you,
in a dry and parched land
> where there is no water. (Psalm 63:1)

Perhaps then I began to comprehend the desire the late Irish poet/writer John O'Donohue expresses for us:

May you come to accept your longing as divine urgency.
May you know the urgency with which God longs
for you.[1]

I think in the summer of 1945 I first realized that what is most deeply personal is also most widely universal. That sense of God caring for a lonely young man was the seed of a desire to help my peers know Christ. It was the voice of my calling—to be an evangelist—a bearer of good news, to invite others into this transforming friendship.

4

CALLED TO LEAD,
LED TO PREACH

The Spirit of the Lord is on me, because
he has anointed me to proclaim good news to the poor . . .
to proclaim freedom for the prisoners.

LUKE 4:18

On an October afternoon I am standing on the edge of Tecumseh Park, back home in Chatham, exactly sixty years plus a month since I left here for college. I have come to preach at the 175th anniversary of our Presbyterian church.

The scarlet maple leaves are glistening after a rain, as I stand and remember sounds from my boyhood. The thwack of a ball in a catcher's mitt. The crack of my dad's fast bowl on the lawn bowling green. "O Canada" played by the Kiltie band concert on a summer evening.

From where I stand, on William Street, I look across at two buildings, remembering two voices from nearby. In that blue stucco house to the left I lay in bed while snow fell silently outside, muffling only slightly my mother's complaining voice, as she and my dad argued deep into the night.

On the corner to the right is the school auditorium where we held our monthly youth rallies. There I heard the arresting voice of a young evangelist who came to speak to a packed crowd, also on a cold wintry night.

Two very different voices. Listening to them helped to shape my life. The voice of my mother. And the voice of Billy Graham.

Billy's Voice

I was sixteen when I first heard Billy Graham at the vast Billy Sunday Tabernacle in Winona Lake, Indiana, for the annual Youth for Christ conference. I was there as leader of the rally in my hometown.

At that time I was dubbed as "the youngest Youth for Christ director in the world." Perhaps so. I was certainly the least experienced.

In the fall of 1945, not long after I had that summer encounter with God in prayer at Blue Water, a man named Evon Hedley came to Chatham to organize a branch of the new Canadian Youth Fellowship, soon to become part of Youth for Christ. A handful of us met with him. We liked the idea he presented and agreed to form a committee.

"You need to have some officers," Evon told us. My friend Danny nominated me as vice president. Evon looked bemused. "You are supposed to have a president first," he told us. So Danny nominated me as president.

Because I was tall, Evon thought I was seventeen. When he learned he had just appointed a fourteen-year-old boy, he must have nearly had a heart attack! But he stuck with me, gave me ideas, sent speakers our way, and let me know if I got things wrong. He was my first mentor, and for his one hundredth birthday, three years before his death, he celebrated with sixty younger men he mentored across the years.

As Evon's mentee and invited as a local leader, I was at the Winona Lake event. That annual Youth for Christ conference included a display—if not a virtual competition—of preachers.

Some were very talented. Their words were gripping. But then there was Billy. He was, as we would say today, "the man," the especially "anointed" one. Most aspiring young preachers wanted to be like him—Billy of the powder-blue, sleek, double-breasted gabardine suit; the floral tie; the flashing eyes; the stabbing forefinger.

The setting fades. His garb has changed. But I still remember that voice.

"Prepare to meet thy God," he would declaim in his rapid-fire style, influenced perhaps from the staccato pace of the newscaster Walter Winchell.

There was a sound of thunder in that voice, but also the softness of a Southern night. His drawn-out vowels and breathy r's gave a hint of Scottish ancestry and North Carolina roots. "Prepaaaahhh," he would warn his hearers. When at the end he invited, *urged*, them to come forward, they almost always did. What was the secret? As one of my preacher buddies drawled, "Billy could simply say 'hymn one hundred' and they would come."

There have been many efforts to explain the success and power of Billy Graham's preaching. Why Billy and not others? Among other things there was a providential meeting of the man and his times, a call for peace with God at the end of a great war, a longing for recovery and a new world.

If I close my eyes I can still hear him preaching in some vast stadium, his hair blowing, his voice young and vigorous. It was clear and compelling, like the whistle of a prairie train across the fields of early morning, carrying a hint of mysterious distances to come, and with a force to ferry your soul across some great river.

I can hear that piercing voice: "The Bible says . . ." as he paced with the open Bible in his outstretched hand. When he said, "You come," people got up and walked down the aisle.

Almost always. But there was a night they didn't, a night I heard a different tone.

Billy came to speak at one of our Youth for Christ rallies. On a cold January night people slid along the icy roads to pack that auditorium a block away from our house.

I was presiding, and we were—I know I was—full of great expectations. We had listened to good speakers before, but with Billy we knew it would be different. Many of my high school contemporaries came. Surely most of them would flock to the front and accept Jesus, I thought.

Billy's sermon was magnetic. But when the invitation was given and the music played, not a person moved. We waited. Silence. Tension. Finally, one young girl came and stood at the front to renew her dedication. We waited again. No one else came forward.

I was devastated, although later that young woman devoted herself to Christian service. But it was not the result I had longed for—a breakthrough of conservative Canadian hearts on a cold night.

The meeting ended. I walked to the wings of the platform and stood behind a curtain, almost in tears. At that moment Billy came over, read my disappointment, and reached out. He put an arm around my shoulder.

"Leighton," he said, "God has given you a burden to see people come to know Christ. If you stay humble, I believe God will use you. And I will pray for you."

Those personal words and that arm around my shoulder have stayed with me far more than his sermon that night. It was the voice of an encourager—and then of an erstwhile matchmaker. When he got back to Charlotte he told his young sister Jean that he had met someone in Canada that he hoped she would meet if she went to Wheaton.

Whether matchmaker or mentor, that disappointing night became the start of a lifelong connection.

Called to Lead and to Preach

Launching that fledgling Youth for Christ movement in my hometown gave me a firsthand chance to learn about leadership and organizing: building a team, writing ads for the paper, booking speakers and musicians, getting people to pray, visiting pastors to get their youth involved, even giving my first real sermon at a small brick church on the north shore of Lake Erie.

That night I chose to speak on the great feast of King Belshazzar, written in the book of Daniel. I described the king proposing a toast to many gods, then seeing a hand writing his doom on the wall.

"The wine glass dropped from his shaking fingers," I said as dramatically as I could. At that moment someone dropped a hymn book on the wooden floor with a crash. Everyone jumped. A friend accused me afterward of planning that for effect. I had not, but he is still convinced I did.

At the end a young Japanese Canadian girl came forward, the only one. But I remember her as the first ever to accept my invitation to Jesus. And, I am moved to realize now, the first of many.

When later in life I came across these words of John Masefield they resonated deeply with the voices I heard in those postwar years.

I did not think, I did not strive,
The deep peace burnt my me alive; . . .
I knew that Christ had given me birth
To brother all the souls on earth.[1]

5

CROSSING NEW THRESHOLDS

Christ, in whom are hidden all the treasures
of wisdom and knowledge.

COLOSSIANS 2:2-3

In late summer of 1949 I drove our family's late-model four-door Buick, blue with a white top, to Wheaton College in Illinois to enter as a sophomore transfer. I was probably the only student to show up in a slick recent model car. Little did the other students know the reason I had a car—not because our family was so well-off but because I was the only one in the family who knew how to drive. My parents had bought a car on my sixteenth birthday so I could drive them around, and they let me take it to Wheaton.

Wheaton had not been in my thinking at all until Billy Graham came to speak at our youth rally. It turned out to be a significant encounter, both for my future ministry and also for a significant change in my educational plans. My mother invited Billy to our house after the meeting for a light supper, and he asked what I would do after I finished high school. I said I was going to the University of Toronto.

"Have you thought about Wheaton College?" he asked. I had read a Wheaton-based novel, *Silver Trumpet*, but otherwise knew little of the school. With his encouragement I decided to apply, and Billy wrote a letter of recommendation.

I was turned down. I may have been the only person Billy Graham ever recommended who was not accepted to Wheaton College! Wheaton's capacity was stretched to the limit with veterans who returned to college after World War II. A few weeks later I met the college president, Dr. Raymond Edman, when he was speaking in Detroit, and told him that I really wanted to attend Wheaton. I was accepted to enroll as a sophomore that same year, receiving one year's credit for grade 13 in the Ontario system.

I crossed many new thresholds when I arrived in Wheaton, first and foremost as an immigrant—a legal one. I applied for a student visa and received a green card with permanent status. I suppose like many immigrants I was a bit in awe. Everything in the United States seemed bigger and faster. It was more like moving to live with distant cousins who had different accents rather than moving to an alien land. The Wheaton students were diverse, including a number of fellow Canadians. We played hockey together. I was the goalie since I had fairly good reflexes but didn't skate too well.

It was one of the significant moves in my life: from a small Canadian city to the environs of Chicago. From a provincial high school to a college filled with war veterans who had experienced the world and its needs firsthand. From contemporaries content to live ordinary lives to friends with larger aspirations. From a troubled family to new freedom. I was excited, nervous, expectant. Suddenly at seventeen, I was thrust into a new world, emotionally, intellectually, socially.

One connection I didn't leave behind: my mother, Olive. She decided she would also move to Wheaton. No other students I knew had their mother move close to the college to watch over them. I didn't advertise her presence. She stayed that first term in a boarding house on the other side of the railway tracks that bisected the town. I went, dutifully, to see her once or twice a week.

Otherwise, my world opened up. I was about to discover something to believe, someone to love, and a cause to live for.

The Life of the Mind

Wheaton's high academic standards attracted me from the beginning. I had come to study and was eager to learn all I could. A few of the required courses were dull and pedestrian. Others were stretching and enriching. They gave me a new and deeper appreciation for the Bible as the book that deeply understood our humanness and the world as the theater of God's glory. I could wish I had been exposed more to classical education and great literature. But what Wheaton offered was stimulating and rewarding.

Philosophy became my area of choice and growth. I strongly desired to be a thinking Christian. Philosophy appealed to me because of the questions it raised about existence itself—and about my own life and faith, my questions and doubts.

Rilke's *Letters to a Young Poet*, which I read much later, would have resonated powerfully with my condition then:

Be patient toward all that is unsolved in your heart and try to love the questions themselves, like locked rooms and like books that are written in a very foreign tongue.... Live the questions now. Perhaps you will then gradually, without noticing it, live along some distant day into the answer.[1]

Young Christians in some circles and in those times were not always encouraged to ask probing questions. Quite the opposite. They were often warned that college might bleach away their faith. But I did have questions—large ones about the universe and personal ones about how to live my own life.

If I was to be an honest and thinking person, I had to face the questions and the doubts. There were times when I was so troubled by unsettling moods that I would climb a tree near the house where I stayed—perhaps seeking a vantage point and a solitary space to survey the world and my own psyche. Perhaps that tree reminded me of trees near my old home in Canada. I would sit there on a branch for an hour or more, wondering about life, feeling the distance from home, from people around, and perhaps at times from God.

I was learning the difference between doubt as intellectual testing and disbelief as a self-aggrandizing refusal to accept what is uncomfortable. At Wheaton I discovered guides on my path through the thicket of uncertainty: my philosophy teachers. They were bright and godly men—Kenneth Kantzer, John Luchies, Arthur Holmes—who thought deeply and lived wisely. They called us to know that *all truth is God's truth* (the title of one of Holmes's books), and that we need not fear exploring truth in whatever way it comes to us and wherever it leads.

Philosophy appealed to me because it demanded a wide and deep view of the world and its connectedness. One of my key strengths seems to be connecting—holding ideas and people together. As I have made my way through the great issues of philosophy, I have come to see how understanding God as tripersonal—one God in three persons, Father, Son, Holy Spirit—sheds light on some of the profound puzzles life presents to us. In philosophy, how are the "many and the one" related? In science, is light a particle or a wave or both? In politics, how do our policies care both for individual needs and the health of society as a whole?

I claim no profound philosophical insights into any of these issues. The questions themselves have moved me to ask: What does it mean to be whole persons? How can we bring people together? How can we connect through our differences?

Through my teachers and reading I progressed enough to get high marks in comprehensive philosophy exams, sufficient for my professors to encourage me to go on to graduate study in the field.

I was flattered by their interest but found that the life of the mind was leading me in another direction. How could thinking Christians best present the claims of faith to thoughtful seekers?

The Life of Love

When Billy Graham wrote a letter on my behalf to Wheaton, he also mentioned that his sister Jean wanted to attend there. My mother picked up on that. Whenever I was interested in a girl, she would say, "You haven't met Billy Graham's sister yet."

She may have thought that would be a worthy match. But deep down she didn't want me to get attached to any girl, at least not for a long, long time. She had other plans for me—and for her.

And that, I now understand, is why she came to Wheaton when I did, not only to protect my interests but her own.

Sometime during my first year, she went back to Canada, not to Chatham but to Toronto, where she found a place to live in the home of a retired police detective and his wife, where she could feel secure and protected from Dad. She was always imagining that he might have her put away in an institution or steal what belonged to her. For the rest of their lives she and Dad lived apart.

When Jeanie arrived at Wheaton a year after I did, we didn't go out of our way to meet. Neither of us wanted to feel pushed into anything. Jeanie certainly wasn't lacking for dates. She says she first noticed me selling popcorn at a basketball game. I saw her from a distance in passing.

Then my Canadian friend, hockey teammate, and erstwhile matchmaker, John Wesley White, made a proposal.

"I have been going out with this farm girl from North Carolina," he told me. "But I don't think she's interested in me. I think you ought to meet her."

John then told Jeanie that she should meet me. He embroidered my assets extravagantly. He told her that I played the piano and the trumpet. (Piano yes, trumpet no). That my parents owned silver mines in Switzerland. (They did sell Swiss watches.) That I lived in a large house on an estate with a river flowing through it. (Our modest house next to the park.)

John's talent for exaggeration was legendary. I doubt Jeanie believed his description of me. She did agree to go with him to a Chicago Black Hawks hockey game on a double date with me and another girl.

I don't remember who won. I do remember that an elderly woman above us cheered so loudly her teeth fell out! Jeanie wondered why I paid more attention to her than to my date. She was impressed, she admits, with the big stylish blue Buick I drove to the game.

I do remember Jeanie. How could I ever forget those eyes, that lovely blond hair, that soft Southern voice, and her humor and warmth? My reserved Canadian heart was totally turned inside out and upside down.

Our first real date was almost a total disaster. I asked her to go to a concert but showed up late. She thought I wasn't coming and was changing her outfit to go to the library. When we got to the concert it was so crowded I couldn't even sit with her. Afterward, I was tongue-tied with shyness. To add to my *faux pas* I got her back to her dorm after curfew so she was "campused"—not allowed to go out at all except to the library—for the whole next weekend.

Somehow I survived that first-date fiasco. We went to church one Sunday night and on the way back stopped at a drive-in café on North Avenue. When I handed her an orange drink, our eyes met, and we connected. I found in her warmth and a safe place that I had longed for. She says she saw in me maturity and purpose years beyond most of the boys she had dated. We were drawn together physically, emotionally, spiritually.

I had planned to return to Canada to theological college or to Princeton Seminary. But falling in love with this Southern girl made me think it would be good to know something about life in the Southern states. Through Ruth Graham's father, Nelson Bell, I learned about Columbia Seminary just outside Atlanta.

Late in the summer of 1952 I visited Columbia, applied, and was admitted.

Going south was a crosscultural experience for this Canadian. My first morning they served grits. I thought it was Cream of Wheat and was astonished they served it on a plate. Cream of Wheat went in a bowl—at least where I came from. The next morning they served Cream of Wheat, and I thought it was grits. I ladled it onto a plate!

Columbia turned out to be a good next step toward ministry, although some of the courses were less challenging than Wheaton. I found that I knew more philosophy and Greek than some students from prestigious schools. Friendships quickly formed that were to last for years. I lived in the same room in which Peter Marshall, the renowned chaplain of the US Senate, had stayed years before. Every other weekend I preached at a small Georgia church. I played on the basketball team and eventually served as president of the student body.

My mother again decided, without asking my opinion, that I needed her nearby. So again she left Ontario and moved to Atlanta. Once more I had to explain or explain away or try to minimize her presence.

That year was hard to be away from Jeanie. We wrote letters every day (letters still stored in our attic). About every two weeks I could afford to call her for three minutes from one of the old-style pay phones. Once or twice I managed to get a ride, or find an excuse, to fly through Chicago for a day or two.

We were very much in love, but Jeanie was not sure that I was going to ask her to marry me. Her final year at Wheaton was passing. We'd dated over two years. She wondered if she should be open to some of the other guys at Wheaton.

Jeanie decided to ask for a clear sign. She prayed that if we were to marry, I would propose before the end of 1952.

During that Christmas break I flew to Charlotte. On New Year's Eve at 11:30 p.m. we sat on a sofa in her parents' farm home on Park Road. I told her a story about a prince who searched all over the world for the "true light" and finally returned home to find that light there in his "true love's eyes." At two minutes to midnight, knowing nothing of her prayer, I knelt and asked, "Will you marry me?"

"I'd love to," she answered. I said, "Let's pray."

I just beat the clock! Jeanie now admits she might have allowed another minute or two of grace if I had missed the midnight deadline. After Jeanie graduated from Wheaton she went to work in two of her brother Billy's crusades while I went to steamy Galveston, Texas, as a summer assistant at First Presbyterian Church. And we made plans to marry.

My mother was totally opposed to my marrying Jeanie. In truth I think she would have opposed my marrying anyone. "Billy Graham's sister" now became her threat, who was taking her son away from God's plan (and hers). She insisted over and over that I had to postpone any thought of marriage until I had finished seminary and completed doctoral studies overseas.

I went to visit Billy at his Montreat, North Carolina, home and told him of the choice I had to make: my mother's demand or my own heart's desire.

"Leighton," he insisted, "if you don't cut those apron strings now you won't ever do it, and you won't be able to live your life as you should."

We set a date. December 19. Two weeks before the wedding the phone rang at the Graham house at two o'clock in the morning, waking up Jeanie and her father. It was my mother, calling Jeanie and instructing her not to marry me.

"You are ruining his life," she insisted.

Jeanie listened as mother went on and on telling her why we shouldn't marry. Then Jeanie firmly said that we would go ahead with our plans. Mother exploded. Jeanie quietly ended the conversation. "I wasn't mad," she remembers now, "but my daddy was, being waked up the middle of the night."

We married as planned, though my mother didn't come. Jeanie's brother Billy married us with a humorous slip of the tongue affirming that we had "exchanged wings." We set out that night for a week-long honeymoon and got as far as the edge of town before I remembered I had forgotten to get gas and had to return to fill up from the Graham farm tank. It was late at night before we headed south to South Carolina and Florida. While she would drive down the road and wait, I would run a mile to get in shape for the coming basketball season. We were so exhausted that we slept most of the time.

Early in the new year, after I recovered from a bout with the flu, we set out for Decatur, Georgia, for life in the seminary. We lived in one room with a bed, a sink, a desk, a bathroom we shared with four other couples, and a Korean student down the hall who sang very loudly early every morning.

In spite of my mother's worries, Jeanie didn't ruin my life. In so many ways we helped each other to grow and mature as persons, as a couple, as servants of the Lord.

We took from the psalms words that expressed our aspiration for life together: "Glorify the LORD with me; let us exalt his name together" (Psalm 34:3).

The Life of Ministry

Those years at Wheaton, and later Columbia, were pivotal for me in a larger sense.

In the early 1950s, evangelical Christianity (known as "conservative" or "fundamentalist") was looked down on as a cultural, social, and intellectual backwater or even (by some cynics) as a swamp. It was a caricature, but a popular one, among the media and intelligentsia.

This takes me back to my Wheaton days when Billy's explosive ministry began. Until then he was not well known outside of Youth for Christ circles. One of my first Sundays at Wheaton I went with friends to hear him preach at the nearby Village Church, where he was pastor. After he finished his sermon he went straight to the airport to fly to Los Angeles to begin a two-week evangelistic campaign, sponsored by a group of Christian laymen.

Soon the Wheaton campus was stirred with news that this annual revival meeting was charged with something new. It was extended week after week. Celebrities (minor but newsworthy ones) were testifying to their newfound faith. The Hearst newspapers featured the young, fiery Southern evangelist, who soon became a national figure. Clippings from stories across the country were posted on our campus bulletin boards.

We were excited. Our newest evangelical hero was big news. The gospel was front page. Revival was happening in our time.

That winter revival hit our own campus during the midwinter spiritual emphasis week. The guest speaker was not a high-velocity preacher like Billy. He was a mild-mannered Philadelphia pastor, who repeated over and over, "Any old ditch can be a channel."

At one evening service, a student stood up and asked for time to confess his failures. Another followed. Then another. That went on for forty-eight hours nonstop. Most of the confessions were for pretty minor offenses—missing chapel, forgetting prayer time, gossip, occasionally something more serious like cheating on an exam. One student even confessed that he told his friends how boring one of his teachers was. We hoped that prof was not there to hear the confession.

As far as I recall, I couldn't think of anything personal that deserved public confession, but I was impressed with the sincerity of those who spoke and the palpable sense of God's presence.

The *Chicago Tribune* heard about what was happening and carried a front-page story. The news spread to other Midwest schools, who experienced their own versions of the collegiate awakenings.

There was no hysteria that week. I remember most the unusual quiet. Along with the personal statements, there was a pervasive sense of joy and connection. "I never saw so many smiles per square face," remarked our president.

After two days and nights, the administration wisely put a hold on the nonstop sessions, the week came to a quiet end, and we resumed our student lives. But we knew something memorable had happened, something beyond what could have been planned or controlled.

Perhaps, we wondered, we were being moved into a new era. One wider and deeper than we could have imagined. Whatever it was, we wanted to be part of it.

I have never experienced that kind of awakening since. What I still recall is a presence that was almost inescapable. Yet for me it was not those intense hours that most nurtured my spirit but quiet hours by myself set aside for prayer and meditation in a room on the second floor of Blanchard Hall, the main building. There I read the spiritual writings of authors like A. W. Tozer and Oswald Chambers.

I found a connection in late-afternoon prayer meetings with a group of friends in a room over the campus gym. We prayed fervently, and loudly enough that a friend now recollects wondering who those guys were he heard praying overhead as he left after a workout.

Authentic revival or renewal—whatever term best describes it—will lead to an outflow and not just warm inner feelings. So with two friends, Peter Deyneka Jr. and Norm Rohrer, we formed a team to go to nearby churches and youth groups to sing and preach. Pete played the piano. He and Norm played trombone duets (with myself at the keyboard). The three of us sang as a trio, and I preached. Almost every weekend we took off in my Buick to go to our engagements in Illinois or Indiana.

We were not permitted to call ourselves an official Wheaton team because we had not been properly auditioned. We went, credentialed or not, because of a sense that we knew something—Someone—that we needed to share. We made a few converts. I am sure we also made a lot of mistakes. We were giving ourselves a crash course in our craft and calling.

In my three years at Wheaton important voices spoke into my life. The calm, thoughtful voices of my teachers. The soft, loving lilt in the voice of Jeanie. The convicting voice of the Spirit, speaking through the powerful voice of a young evangelist in a tent in Los Angeles, and the quiet voice of an ordinary pastor in our college chapel.

N. T. Wright in *Simply Christian* has described how in our longings for justice, spirituality, relationship, and beauty we hear "the echoes of a Voice."[2] Why do I recall these particular voices and not the many others of those years? As British author Penelope Lively writes in her memoir, *Dancing Fish and Ammonites*, we make a choice of "accessible memories" and are not really able to choose which to remember and which not.[3] If I could retrieve a whole different set of memories, would my Wheaton days have a different cast? Others who were there might recall a very different tableau.

I wasn't self-consciously trying to be something—thinker, lover, leader—although the idea of being a preaching evangelist was forming.

But the three voices I highlight—of the mind, of love, of calling—stay with me because they drew into me and through me and out of me threads that have stitched my life.

From my philosophy classes I retain major ideas of some of the great figures. But the power of questions to stir and enlarge, and the power of truth to guide and anchor our lives, stay with me.

The allure of romantic love and physical attraction between Jeanie and me has stayed, the deep quality of love to connect through the heights and depths of life together.

And the conviction remains that words—spoken words, whether forceful or quiet—have a power to convert, convince, and create.

Through these voices of my student years I was hearing that other Voice, the one poet Mary Oliver calls the "incomparable voice," with tones that continue to resound in the voice of my calling.[4]

6

THE MENTOR AND
THE MOCKINGBIRD

No more boasting about human leaders! All things are yours . . .
and you are of Christ, and Christ is of God.

1 CORINTHIANS 3:21, 23

The poet Mary Oliver describes the mockingbird as "the thief of other sounds," imitating train whistles and truck brakes and the songs of other birds. She had to listen a long time, she says, for "the softer voice of his own life / to come through."[1]

When we are young we too may be mockingbirds, finding models to guide our early steps. Young athletes mimic their heroes, the way they drive to the hoop and shoot a basketball, the way they so gracefully figure skate.

Early in life we may try to find ourselves by pasting on bits and pieces of other people as if we were trying on various personas. But as we desire to become more real and authentic we grow both in and out of those bits and pieces. As the young David cast off Saul's armor when he went to fight Goliath, we begin to integrate what fits into our own person. We discover how, in reflecting Christ, our own truest self is also revealed, so that we can say with the poet Gerard Manley Hopkins, "What I do is me, for that I came."[2]

In high school I had won some oratorical contests, which gave me a head start in public speaking. Then Billy provided the inspiration and the model. Like many young would-be preachers of my generation, I wanted to do it like Billy—following his cadence, copying his gestures.

Even though our accents differed (Canadian versus Southern) people remarked on the similarity of our delivery. Some may have regarded my preaching as imitation. Yet one of Billy's contemporaries said I reminded him so much of Billy (we had the same build) before I had hardly ever heard Billy preach.

He was, early on, my model and a superb one. Across the years he was an encourager, not trying to shape me in his image but allowing me to become true to what I was called to be.

The Bible is replete with instances of what we today might call mentoring relationships, of elders passing the torch of leadership to the younger. Moses taking his young aide Joshua with him for the most intimate encounters with God. Elijah's cloak falling on Elisha's shoulders. Eli the priest helping young Samuel discern God's voice.

A classic example is Paul taking young Timothy with him as a companion in ministry. I am especially impressed with what Paul wrote to his "dear son": "I remind you to fan into flame the gift of God, which is in you through the laying on of my hands" (2 Timothy 1:6).

Others have translated those words as exhorting Timothy to "stir up the gift," to "stir up the inner fire," to "keep it ablaze."

Paul's striking words describe this spiritual gift as

- *Initiated* as "the gift of God"—not originated by ourselves.
- *Mediated* by Paul and the elders—"through the laying on of . . . hands."
- *Stimulated* by Timothy himself—he was to "fan [it] into flame" by using it.

Paul's urging of his protégé is perhaps the way most of us find our gift and our way. God's call comes in part through the discernment of someone else, perhaps a veteran like Paul, ignites a spark in our imagination, and then is realized in practice.

It certainly was a gift for me to have my brother-in-law, Billy, as a model, mentor, and caring shepherd.

He was the affirming mentor when he invited me to join his evangelistic team for a year and then asked me to go to New York to recruit the support of pastors and churches for his historic sixteen-week crusade in Madison Square. I wonder, if I'd been in his place, would I have entrusted that project to a twenty-four-year-old just out of seminary?

—◌◌◌—

Our relationship in those days was not especially up close and personal. We didn't often have long talks about ministry and theology and issues. I could wish, looking back, we had been closer. But I was shy and somewhat intimidated by him, and he was busy with his preaching and planning. I was able to learn by sitting on the platform and listening to him preach, watching him from a distance. Occasionally, he would invite me to sit in on a private lunch with civic leaders. I listened and watched as he tactfully brought Christ into the conversation.

Billy had an inner team who had been with him from the start of his crusades. Some of them were friends from his growing-up years. There was a wider group of associates who came and went. I was somewhere in between, neither an intimate nor out on the edge.

I think he never quite knew how to relate to me, although he would ask my opinion on issues and entrust major responsibilities to me across the years. I know he valued my help. For a while he may have thought I would succeed him in leading his organization, which was never my ambition. But there was never a really good fit between myself and others of his close associates who had been with him for years. And my own take on some social issues was regarded as perhaps too "liberal".

We teamed up frequently in those early years, especially in other countries. I would go to a city in Africa, the Caribbean, and Europe to preach for a week or more, with Billy speaking at the closing rallies.

After I had been with him as an associate evangelist for a half dozen years, he asked me to drive up to his mountain home. He told me he had been thinking and praying about my future ministry and thought it would be good if I formed my own team and focused my evangelistic preaching in cities across Canada. He suggested I could either form a new organization that he would support or do this as part of his own association.

Jeanie and I thought and prayed about this. There was some appeal in going out on my own, partly because I sensed that some of his team were ambivalent if not envious of my relationship to Billy. He may have thought it would be better for me in the long run to lead my own ministry and develop my gifts. And in this he may have been right.

During these years he also from time to time suggested other leadership roles for me—to edit *Christianity Today* or head a seminary—attractive ideas to be sure. They were not what I sensed to be my calling. But I was grateful for his confidence.

In any case I decided to take up his offer and form a new team within the Graham association. This would provide me a platform without having to build a whole new organization and allow me to lead evangelism efforts across Canada and other parts of the world. Our teamwork had fruitful results and sometimes humorous moments.

One of my Canadian crusades (as they were then called) was in Halifax, the capital of Nova Scotia. I preached for two weeks with Billy arriving to speak the final weekend.

The last rallies were outdoors on Citadel Hill in the center of the city.

Billy arrived a day early and sat at the back of the crowd on the grass. As I finished preaching and invited people to come forward as a sign of their trust in Christ, Billy (as he told me later) saw an older man just in front of him squirming, obviously uncomfortable.

Assuming that the man was convicted by the message and struggling, Billy decided to do a little personal evangelism. He leaned forward, tapped the man on the shoulder, and asked if he wanted to go down and give his life to Christ.

The old fellow turned, and, not recognizing Billy, who was wearing dark glasses, thought a moment, then said, "Nah, I think I'll wait until the big gun comes tomorrow night!"

Voices Together yet Different

There's an old rabbinical story about Rabbi Zusma, who said, "When I stand before God, he will not ask: why were you not Moses? He will ask: why were you not Zusma?"

My relationship with Billy allowed me to observe and learn from a master communicator, yet have space to find my own voice.

Billy and I had the same passion to make Christ known. Yet we were different in various ways: in personality, background, and experiences. But the important question was not how we differed but how God had shaped each of us for our callings.

Up to a point I was flattered when people who listened to the "Hour of Decision" broadcast, on which I alternated week by week with Billy, would say they couldn't tell much difference between Billy and me. Up to a point. But then the need to develop my own authentic voice emerged.

I have an ability, it seems, to connect ideas and people. It has made me a networker of people and also brought a longing to see God's world and work in Christ in all its wholeness. I needed to understand evangelism in terms of a larger vision beyond assembling crowds and calling for decisions. Public proclamation was and is for me a joy and a holy calling. It was also part of a larger whole.

As I wrote in my first book, *The Christian Persuader*, evangelism is not a one-time encounter but the calling of the whole church to embody and proclaim the whole gospel for the whole world.

I had this inner passion to live this wholeness out in my own calling, both in how I did the work of an evangelist and how I thought and wrote about it.

I was inspired by the maxim of an old Scottish theologian, James Denney, who believed that "if evangelists were our theologians, or theologians our evangelists, we should come nearer being the ideal church."[3]

And Billy warmly affirmed this part of my calling.

In another way there was a singular change. When, early on, I learned from and in a sense "took on" Billy's voice, I also submerged part of my own.

Yet in the ways that rivers course and curve and turn back on themselves and flow on, I found a way to rediscover deep channels that had been quietly waiting to be filled.

As the years passed, my voice began to take on a tone that was different—not at the center, in the heart and truth of the gospel, but in the angles, in my way of uttering that gospel.

My style became a bit softer, more conversational, perhaps more thoughtful, more talking *with* than talking *to* people, always knowing that it is the Lord's Voice—not mine or ours—that carries the authority.

This came home to me powerfully many years ago in Australia. I was invited to a country town (with the exotic name Wagga Wagga) to speak at an early-morning gathering of Royal Australian Air Force recruits in training.

The evening before, I spoke at an open-air rally. It was wet and cold, and I became hoarse. By the morning my voice was almost totally gone as I went to the hangar where the recruits had gathered.

An airport hangar is about the worst place imaginable for acoustics, all metal structure and cement floor. When I rose to speak the microphone was down too low. I lifted it up and the connecting wire broke. What to do? I could hardly say a word.

Somehow for several minutes I spoke (or rather croaked!), explaining the gospel as simply as I could until my voice gave out entirely. I left the platform disheartened. What a great opportunity it was to present Christ to hundreds of young men, most of whom had no connection with the church at all, and I had blown it.

A few days later the padre, chaplain at that base, came to Sydney and located me at one of Billy's rallies. "Leighton," he said, "I know it was hard for you to speak. But over this past week at least twenty-five of those young men have come to my office, asking how they can come to know Christ."

It was a lesson hard learned: God does not depend on my voice.

As I was asked to preach in various countries and different settings, I learned to listen more to voices from those cultures— the voices of new believers who coined fresh words and songs to express their newfound faith, of secular novelists and social activists, even of some theologians who were asking important questions even though they jettisoned profound biblical truth.

Were there times of questioning? Even of doubt? Yes, though more about my own inadequacies than about God. And those times brought me back again and again to what Paul exclaimed to be "the depth of the riches of the wisdom and knowledge of God" (Romans 11:33).

I began to see how Christ is like a beautiful diamond, a gem of great value, with many facets. So Asians may see in Christ a truth that Europeans miss, and Africans may see reflected in him a loveliness that North Americans overlook. It takes a whole world to even begin to see all the treasures there are in our Lord.

It also takes many leaders and mentors to draw us to the fullness that is found only in Christ. Paul has these wise words: "No more boasting about human leaders! All things are yours . . . and you are of Christ, and Christ is of God" (1 Corinthians 3:21, 23).

All mentors and mentees should take those words to heart.

And I can say to the Lord: *Thanks for giving dear Billy a voice to the nations, one that invited me alongside. For all he meant, thanks. And for all you have called me to be: praise!*

The Sound of Billy's Voice

Billy Graham's public voice was widely heard and stirring. What was not overheard but what I most fondly remember is the caring, private voice.

I remember his breaking voice, choking back tears, as he spoke at the funeral of our son Sandy, who died during heart surgery when he was twenty-one.

There was his caring voice to our younger son, Kevin, who that weekend was at a Young Life gathering in the mountains. Billy was the one who drove to tell Kevin that his brother had died, took him home for the night, and drove him back to Charlotte.

Many years later there was the tender voice of an uncle to our Debbie, who had a recurrence of breast cancer and was at Mayo Clinic for tests, dreading that the disease might have spread. Unknown to her, Billy was there for a checkup. When she went for her next test, he was waiting for her at the end of a long hall. She saw at first only an old man in a wheelchair. Then she recognized her uncle and threw herself into his arms. Billy, for whom tears never came easily, cried with her, prayed, and held her.

Later at his home, sitting on his bed, she said, "Uncle Billy, I have heard you preach to big crowds. But as far as I am concerned that was the best sermon you ever preached. It was not you on a platform speaking to a crowd but both of us in our weakness, me so afraid, and you in a wheelchair with no one to observe."

———

My wife, Jeanie, and I were on one of our later visits to her brother. Billy's voice was quiet, his words slow and sometimes tender. His eyes were weak, and his hearing almost totally gone, yet his mind was still clear.

He lay on his bed, his white hair long and lank on the pillow, a throw over his torso. His dogs stayed by him, and the cat named Cat stretched out on the bed. Billy gazed with an almost painful longing at the photo of his beloved and much younger Ruth on the far wall.

When we asked if he would like Jeanie to speak at his funeral and what he would like her to say, he pondered, then said, "He tried to do what he thought he should." And what, I asked, was that? "Preach the gospel."

As we listened to his frail voice, Jeanie thought back to the first time she heard him preach. He was home from Bible school. She was five years old and sat in the balcony at the old Sharon Presbyterian Church with her mother and their maid. She remembered he spoke so loudly she covered her ears with her hands to the great embarrassment of Mother Graham.

I reminded him of that long-ago winter night in Chatham and told him I had never forgotten how he put his arm around me and encouraged me.

There was a pause. And then a weak response, "Praise the Lord."

7

DISCERNING A SHIFT

After the earthquake came a fire, but the LORD was not in the fire.
And after the fire came a gentle whisper.

1 KINGS 19:12

The room was moving! My bed was moving! Everything was moving!

On an early morning in the mid-1960s I was asleep in the Universal Sheraton Hotel in Los Angeles. That morning I was shaken awake with a sense that everything was moving, my bed and the whole room. There was no fixed point of reference. Instinctively, I grabbed the frame of my bed and held on and said a morning prayer, very heartfelt, like, "Help!"

"What's happening?" I called to the hotel operator when the first shaking stopped.

"Oh, we have a little earthquake down here," was her laconic reply.

"Yes, we have one up here too. What should we do? Evacuate?"

"No," she said, "just stay there. If anything more happens the whole place will go."

Obviously, the hotel people had trained their staff to be reassuring!

I was not about to stay up on the eleventh floor. Still in my pajamas, I began to find my way down the hotel stairs, skirting fallen plaster and debris. Outside I stood near the swimming pool, half emptied of water by the quake, and gazed up.

"How do they make buildings to withstand that kind of shaking?" I wondered out loud.

"Two ways," said the man next to me, who had also rushed from the hotel. "The foundations of high rises have to be built down to bedrock. Maybe sixty to a hundred feet down. And the buildings have to be prestressed, with give-and-take in the joints, to allow them to flex under pressure. If they were too rigid they would shatter." He pointed up. "The top was probably swaying ten to twelve feet with the shocks. Otherwise, it would likely have fallen."

I breathed a quiet thanks for engineers.

Later, as I reflected on the earthquake, I thought of life under pressure. Without firm foundations—as in Jesus' parable of houses built on rock, not sand—our lives and our societies could not stand. But equally, without flexibility, the ability to adjust to changing pressures, we and our worlds might also collapse.

We need both the firm assurance of God's sure Word ("We must pay the most careful attention, therefore, to what we have heard" [Hebrews 2:1]) and the movements of the Holy Spirit to guide us into God's new directions.

As the writer of Hebrews says, "At that time his voice shook the earth, but now he has promised, 'Once more I will shake not only the earth but also the heavens . . . so that what cannot be shaken may remain.'" (Hebrews 12:26-27).

After the Earthquake a Still, Small Voice

So it may be after some great cataclysm, when we are searching for security and direction, that we are more attuned to listen for God's voice, perhaps because we are shocked enough to stop and listen.

The prophet Elijah endured an earthquake after a turbulent time in Israel. He had survived a showdown with the false prophets of Baal on Mount Carmel and then fled to the desert to escape the vengeance of Queen Jezebel. Exhausted, he fell into a deep sleep. When he woke, he walked forty days to Mount Horeb. There God asked, "What are you doing here, Elijah?" (1 Kings 19:13). God told Elijah to stand on the mountain and watch.

On that high place Elijah watched a storm go by—a great and powerful wind, an earthquake, fire. At last a "gentle whisper" (or in the familiar King James translation "a still, small voice") brought to him a renewed call and a refreshed sense of God's presence even while so much changed.

That California earthquake was for me a kind of precursor of the shaking which was to come. Across the Western world, but especially in American society, it would break out in civil unrest, demonstrations in the streets against the fault lines of racial injustice and deeply ingrained poverty, and opposition to the Vietnam War.

I was aware of these rumblings of discontent. I had a growing concern for issues of social justice. But since most of my ministry for a decade had taken me outside the United States to Canada,

Australia, and other countries, the issues preoccupying the American scene had not touched me as deeply.

The earthquake marked a time of beginning to listen in a new way to God's whisper. I began to sense some disturbing voices— from the streets and in my own soul—a shaking of some of my own securities. I woke up to realities beyond my own comfort zone.

Disturbing Voices from the Edges

Two blocks from home, in our small and placid city of Chatham, was a terminus of the Underground Railway by which escaping slaves made their way to freedom. Although we Canadians were proud of our tolerance, we had our own prejudices. We had to look for a long time to find a hotel that would accommodate the black gospel "Eureka Jubilee Singers" when they came to perform at our youth rally. In nearby Dresden (now the location of a visitor center dedicated to the underground railway, with a model of the "original" Uncle Tom's cabin), we heard that black people were beaten with bicycle chains in some incidents of racial animosity. But we felt fairly insulated from the pangs of big brother America to the south.

Although Wheaton College was founded as an antislavery school, during my years there I recall little talk about race issues. We had only a handful of African American students. Later at Atlanta's Columbia Seminary there was an ongoing and heated debate over the possible reunion of the southern and northern branches of the Presbyterian churches. The two branches had been split ever since the Civil War. The debates were in part over theology and interpretation of the Bible. But underneath were the fears of change and the longings for freedom, the privileged social patterns of the Old South versus the cry for freedom and civil rights.

As I think back now to my three years in Atlanta, I am astounded how little attention most of us seminarians paid to the injustice of segregation. In Atlanta a future governor and his white customers would chase blacks out of his restaurant with a gun and ax handles. Also in Atlanta a young pastor named Martin Luther King Jr. was beginning his ministry. Meanwhile we seminarians probably spent more time debating and defending the Bible's authority than being scorched by its demands for justice and neighbor love.

Yet I knew instinctively (and from my reading of the Bible) that racism was a sin and a violation of God's purpose, and that all people were created "from one blood." When I entered into full-time ministry I was caught up by the vision of evangelism that aimed not only at converting individuals but also called us to a reconciling gospel.

Billy Graham had taken bold action to desegregate his crusades in the early 1950s. When I joined his team and helped lay the groundwork for his crusades, part of my mandate was to reach out to meet, involve, and befriend leaders from ethnically diverse churches.

The 1957 New York crusade was a shaping time for me. A year before the crusade Jeanie and I lived in Manhattan. Most days I went by car and subway to visit scores of churches and meet hundreds of pastors in the city and surrounding areas from all denominations and all races.

Some of Billy's strongest supporters were leaders of large African American congregations. Other congregations questioned the depth of Billy's stance on racial issues. When I met with the executive pastor of the famous (and famously liberal) Riverside Church, he fixed a stony gaze on me and asked bluntly, "Just how much do you want Negro participation in your 'crusade'?" I stammered an answer about wanting them involved as much as they wanted to be. But I left with my conscience pricked.

Nevertheless, that New York crusade was a kind of watershed in our working with churches of many shades (I use the word intentionally) of theology and diversity. As Billy said, he welcomed and invited participation by all who would support the message he preached. In sociological terms, the crusade was not a "bounded set," defined by excluding walls at the edges, but a "centered set," defined by Christ at the center. It was not about who could be in but who wanted to join in reaching out.

Early that summer of 1957, at Billy's request, I sent a telegram to Martin Luther King Jr., inviting him to speak at the Madison Square Garden crusade. Dr. King, by then a nationally known activist for civil rights, accepted. Jeanie and I met him in the lobby of our hotel and then chatted with him in Billy's private room before we went to the platform. He was pleasant and a bit reserved. We joined with the thousands who packed the Garden that night as Dr. King led us all in prayer. It was the only time I had personal contact with King and the only time he appeared at one of Billy's crusade meetings. I am glad to have played a small part in the meeting between these two leaders. They met on a number of other occasions, and Dr. King asked Billy to call him Mike, as his friends did. They encouraged each other in their efforts. And they remained amiable though not close friends.

How, I wonder now, might our racial history be different if more evangelical leaders had followed Billy's lead and joined the gospel call for personal salvation with the kingdom call for justice and reconciliation?

Around that time I began to hold my own crusades around the world. I met and was deeply impressed by evangelists who combined preaching and social concern—like Tom Allan of Scotland, Joe Blinco of the British Methodists, and Alan Walker of Australia. They became role models for me. Pioneering evangelical activists, such as John Perkins of the Voice of Calvary in rural Mississippi, inspired me to listen to the voices of prophets being raised again.

Yet with all this I needed to feel personally and deeply touched by how discrimination and poverty devalued people. Perhaps, like the apostle Peter, I was a slow learner. Peter knew Jesus, was forgiven, and preached the gospel with power. But he still thought Gentiles, or non-Jews, were "unclean." It took a dream, a visitation by an angel, and an encounter with a God-fearing Gentile soldier named Cornelius to make Peter understand the reconciling reality of the gospel. When Peter entered this Gentile soldier's house, his first words were not a sermon to Cornelius but a confession of his own need: "God has shown me that I should not call anyone impure or unclean" (Acts 10:28).

It took the voices of others—Enoch Fears, Ed Pratt, and some hippies whose names I never knew—to bring God's call for justice and reconciliation home strongly to my own conscience.

Enoch Fears was an African American airman on his way to Vietnam. He came to a Presbyterian church where I was assigned to preach in Montgomery, Alabama, when I visited Billy's crusade there in the early sixties.

What I did not know, until after the service, was that Fears was turned away by the "greeters." Several other African Americans arrived at the same time. The church leaders had agreed that if more than one black person at a time tried to enter it was a sign they were coming to protest, not to worship. Their policy was to turn groups of blacks away. I had no knowledge of their policy and later made a public statement that I would never preach in a segregated audience. Still later I had a friend deliver a letter of apology to Enoch Fears in Vietnam. I never heard from him, never met him, but my conscience was stung—as it should have been.

The incident was reported fairly widely, especially in some of the Presbyterian publications, and the congregation was both heatedly criticized and defended.

I felt chagrined, embarrassed, and deeply offended—for Enoch Fears, for the crusade, for the gospel. I felt ashamed. My sermon that day was about Jesus coming "to seek and save" the lost and the outsiders. But clearly the *point* of the sermon was lost. How could an excluding church represent an including Lord?

My shakeup continued through Ed Pratt. Ed was the director of the Urban League in Seattle when I went to lead a citywide campaign there in 1968. Pratt agreed to give me a tour of the inner city so I could see firsthand some of the challenges the city faced. Seattle was generally known as a progressive city, but that day Ed Pratt showed me the other side—substandard housing, unemployment, the de facto patterns of segregation.

After the tour I asked what the churches in Seattle were doing to help.

He stared straight into my eyes as he said, "Reverend, the church has moved only when it has been run over from behind." Words I have never forgotten.

The next winter Ed Pratt heard a snowball thrown against his house. He opened the door to see who it was and was killed by a shotgun blast. His murder has never been solved. His voice was silenced. But his words stayed with me. I knew we had to call people both to personal faith in Christ and to faithful, caring action in his name.

A New Conviction in Seattle

After my conversation with Ed Pratt, our team and the local campaign leaders prayed and took some small but significant steps. At the crusade service we invited some lay activists to share their personal faith stories. They would testify not only of finding forgiveness in Christ but of heeding a call to action. A newspaper reporter told about coming to faith in Christ and also about his call to start a ministry in local jails. Others told of providing jobs and housing to the working poor.

I would end with an invitation for people to come forward to open their lives to Christ. But also I would explain that "Help Tables" were set up in the lobby, representing local service agencies. Those who sensed the Lord calling them to put their faith to work should sign up to help.

The Seattle effort was modest in terms of numbers, but it marked a renewed call for me to emphasize the revolutionary character of the gospel, to quote both prophets like Amos ("let justice roll down") and evangelists like John ("whoever will may come").

As I preached, with Bible in my hand, people seemed to listen and to realize the gospel could not be reduced to an either-or—personal faith or social concern. Both justification by faith and justice pursued are on God's kingdom agenda.

God's disturbing voice got to me most powerfully through voices, as it were, from the edges.

An Eruption in Minneapolis

As this emphasis on faith in action became a feature of our outreach events, it attracted publicity. The wedding of evangelism and social concern seemed novel, even heretical to some, although it was in truth a recovery of long biblical and historical roots. *Christianity Today* and other publications began to carry stories about this "innovation."

When the US Congress on Evangelism was held in Minneapolis, I was invited to bring a keynote message on "The Church and Evangelism in a Day of Revolution."

I began by comparing our world to Jeremiah's vision of a "boiling pot and seething cauldron"—an age of constant, rapid, pervasive change, not of isolated revolt but of total revolution.

I concluded, "God's revolution is going to go on, without you and me. But I don't want to get left behind. So this is my prayer: 'Lord, start a revolution, and start it in me!'"

When I finished there was an immediate and enthusiastic response with a standing ovation. The chairman asked Billy Graham for a comment. He strode to the podium and said, "Amen!"

Afterward, many, especially younger leaders, lined up to express thanks and say they had been waiting for someone to speak for them. I was gratified. But I was also dressed down by a very angry man, an official of the National Council of Churches, who was almost shaking as he asked what gave me the right to speak on this topic, that I had no wounds to show.

What had I suffered for social justice? What had the evangelical churches suffered? I was chastened and had to admit our rhetoric was far ahead of our actions.

The next day the broadcaster Paul Harvey announced on his syndicated and widely heard newscast that "Billy Graham and Leighton Ford have split." His take was that I had turned "liberal" and was preaching "the social gospel." Harvey and Billy were close friends, and his national influence was considerable. His words surely caused consternation for many of his conservative listeners, wondering if Billy and I really were at odds. I sent Harvey a copy of my address and told him that Billy himself said "Amen." Some time later Paul called our house and told Jeanie he was mistaken, and he expressed his regrets. But his words caused some suspicion about whether I was wandering away from the evangelical faith.

The following evening the Minneapolis hall was packed and the atmosphere charged. There was a buzz of expectation carried over from the earlier session. We were looking forward to hearing the popular lay leader and writer Keith Miller. Just as he was introduced, several hippie-looking people walked to the front and sat on the floor just below the stage. Quickly the security people escorted them out.

An immediate burst of protests came from the audience. Keith Miller was angered and burst out, "They just threw out the people here who look most like Jesus."

From where I sat with friends high and off to the side in the balcony of the old Minneapolis Auditorium I could feel the shock of the audience. It was clear that anger could erupt and damage the spirit of the week. Something—a voice from inside—told me not to sit and let this happen. On a sudden impulse I stood up and said, "Let's go and see what we can do about this."

Several friends came with me as we wound our way down to the main floor and learned that the hippies had been taken to the basement. We found stairs down to a cubicle where the group was being questioned by local security people. I told them who we were, and asked what was happening.

"We just came to hear what was going on," said one. He threw up his hands. "We didn't come to cause trouble. We couldn't find good seats so we sat down at the front, up close where we could have a good view."

"I'm sorry they made you leave," I said, and made a quick decision. "Come with me. They'll let you in if we go together." They looked dubious but agreed. As we walked back in with our unexpected "guests," there was a warm burst of welcome, and we sat together on the floor until the evening was over.

Many welcomed the hippies after the evening was over and apologized that they had earlier been turned out. A few leaders were upset because they felt security had been breached.

A friend later asked me what I had been thinking when I got up and reached out to the hippies.

"I don't remember thinking at all," I said. "There was just an inner sense that a wrong had been done. A growing sense of what the gospel is all about. I don't think I could have sat there and done nothing."

But there was little elation. Perhaps I was remembering the airman who had been turned away in Montgomery. Perhaps it was a realization that we live this life in Christ, not from the top down but from the ground up, with the Christ who came among us, moved into the neighborhood—into the "hood" we might say today—who walked the streets and ate dinner with sinners whether poor and lowly or high and mighty.

A voice was calling me down, that the way of the kingdom is not ascent but descent.

Perhaps, through the voices of Enoch Fears, Ed Pratt, and those hippies, it was that same still, quiet voice that Elijah heard asking, "What are you doing here?"

8

VOICES IN A DARK NIGHT

Out of the depths I cry to you, LORD.

PSALM 130:1

One winter night in 1967, God died—or so it felt. During the rocking sixties, some avant-garde theologians had made quite a stir with their pronouncements on "the death of God." *Time* magazine had even announced God's demise on its front cover. I had scoffed at them. But now I knew exactly when and where he died. It was on a flight from Seattle to Charlotte.

Of course it was my faith that faded, not God, but still my sense of loss was very acute.

I had been to Seattle to speak at some preliminary rallies for the major outreach we would launch that year. It was the first time I had been the main speaker in a large American city. I felt extra pressure to do well.

Instead, nothing was going well.

Churches were slow to respond. The finance committee struggled to raise funds. Gaining public attention in a large and secular city was a daunting challenge.

I felt deeply disheartened.

Months before I had been preaching in Regina, Saskatchewan, and had tea with the local Anglican bishop. He was a friendly man, and we had an affable conversation as we talked about our ministries.

"But I do have a problem with you evangelists," he said. "Your reports are always about your successes. Don't you ever have a failure?"

I assured him that we had our less than successful times. But his words stayed with me.

So I wrote to him from Seattle to say, "Bishop, I think I will have a failure to report."

Jeanie's Hands

I sat on that long flight home from Seattle to Charlotte, brooding over my feelings of discouragement and inadequacy.

The fear of failure had haunted me from early years. I can remember as a youngster fleeing from a spelling contest in tears when I missed one word. My mother had branded me with the idea that we were "better than" others. So I always had to be better than everyone else at anything.

(Flash forward to a scene from my later years, when I had begun to paint. The first morning of a weekend workshop in the North Carolina mountains I found myself surrounded by professional artists and experienced amateurs who were extremely gifted. I was so discouraged with my paltry efforts I went outside, sat on a hill, and almost packed up to go home. Fifty years had passed, and I still had to be "better than"!)

It felt as if some inner earthquake was shaking my certainties. Now, I can see that God was trying to get my attention. He was calling me to listen more attentively to his inner voice of love.

On that flight home from Seattle I began to wonder about the future. A former evangelist hero of mine, Chuck Templeton, had left his ministry when he realized he did not himself believe the message he was preaching to others.

If God were dead—or at least if my faith was in tatters—would I have to do the same? Should I quit?

Jeanie met me at the airport that evening and sensed immediately that something was wrong. When the children were asleep we lay down next to each other in our upstairs bedroom. I haltingly told her of the overwhelming feeling that God was absent and how I felt crushed by the weight of it. I let out my confusion and hurt as we talked deep into the night.

"What am I going to do? I can't continue ministry and preaching if God is dead—at least to me. What will I do? What will happen to our team? What will they do?"

Jeanie listened quietly, offered a few gentle questions and suggestions, and then gave up trying to analyze. Sometime after midnight she reached out her hands, one on each side of my face, and said over and over, "I love you. I love you. I love you." Her touch on my skin and her words in my heart got me through.

At that painful time, Jeanie's hands carried God's voice. It was the echo of Jesus' call, "Come to me, all who labor and are heavy laden, and I will give you rest" (Matthew 11:28 RSV).

There would be times to come when I would need those hands, that voice, again.

———⌇———

I had thirty minutes to face my inner monster. In half an hour I had to leave my room and go to speak to the students at the University of Tulsa. But I was scared to death, too afraid to leave my room.

What was I to do? What was happening to me?

In spring of 1975 I had gone to Los Angeles to address a gathering of national evangelical leaders. For some reason I was uptight and nervous and felt that my speech had not connected. At least it was not up to what I had wanted it to be.

From there I went straight to Tulsa to begin a preaching series. I suddenly found myself seized by a sense of inadequacy. Darkness seized me and would not let go.

Across the years I had made many outward journeys in my travels around the world to so many places and people. Now I needed to make an inward and downward journey. That meant going into some dark places.

The educator Parker Palmer writes that true and authentic leadership comes from those who have made a downward journey. They have gone into the dark places "where the monsters are" and only then can help others into the light.

I read Parker Palmer's description of his own inward and downward journey through an extended depression. The well-meaning advice of friends didn't help. Antidepressants gave only limited relief. He felt at times totally disengaged from life.

Two things helped. One was a friend who came by in late afternoons and without conversation simply massaged his feet. The other was a therapist who offered an image that reframed his sense of what was going on.

"You seem to look upon depression as the hand of an enemy trying to crush you," he said to Palmer. "Could you see it instead as the hand of a friend, pressing you down to ground upon which it is safe to stand?"

With that image, Palmer began to look at depression as a friend who had been following him for years, calling out his name, tapping him on the shoulder. But not until this friend reached out and literally "de-pressed" him to the ground did he come to realize that the way to God—and to discovering his true calling—was down.

In a paradox of the spiritual life he found that "the humiliation that brings us down—down to ground on which it is safe to stand or fall—eventually takes us to a finer and fuller sense of self."[1]

Biblical figures like the prophets Elijah and Jonah made these journeys. For Elijah it came after his showdown with the false prophets and having to run from Queen Jezebel's murderous intent. For Jonah it happened when the city of Nineveh quickly repented at his preaching and his mission was ended. They both became so depressed they asked God to let them die.

Ordinarily, my moods can go up as quickly as they descend. The dark times I went through in the 1960s did not last long. Light reappeared. But the darkness lurked and in the mid-1970s returned. Perhaps I had kept it at a distance with my busyness. This time it was out of the need to sustain success.

Mistaking Adrenaline for the Holy Spirit

It seemed everything was going well. I was totally immersed in my calling—preaching around the world, writing my first book, lecturing at seminaries. I recorded regularly a message for the "Hour of Decision" and produced a daily inspirational TV feature. I chaired the program for the groundbreaking Lausanne Congress on World Evangelization.

I was reveling in the delights and challenges of our children. There were basketball games to coach for the boys. Long walks and talks with Debbie about friends and future.

It was a productive season. I was too busy to pay attention to my inner needs.

The psychologist Arch Hart shared an insight that has stayed with me: "A lot of young leaders mistake the high they get from adrenaline as coming from the Holy Spirit. And when that adrenaline rush goes down they think the Spirit has gone."

I sense that I made that mistake. I was not aware of how stressed out I was.

Many people assumed I was being groomed to succeed Billy Graham. Although I wasn't aiming to succeed him, I was exhausted from the pressure of trying to live up to everyone's expectations, including my own.

When I arrived in Tulsa for that preaching series, I was supposed to meet the local committee for breakfast the first morning. I made some excuse and did not go.

I did not want to be with people. For the first few nights of our rallies I had to force myself to walk to the podium and speak. I felt nothing I had to say would matter to anyone. I uttered the correct words but with no inner grip, no "anointing" as the old preachers would say. It was not doubt about the truth of the message that consumed me. I even knew that people were helped. It was I, the messenger, who felt as if I were removed, on the outside, looking at myself and them from a distance.

I told the core of our team what I was going through, and they were sympathetic and encouraging but puzzled.

Then came that morning when I was scheduled to speak at the university. I was petrified. Open-air gatherings in university could be hostile. What questions would be hurled that I could not answer? How many catcalls might come? How would I respond?

I knew I had to go. I didn't know how I could do it. Alone in my oppressive hotel room, I knelt and spoke to God as honestly as I could about my panic.

"I am afraid of what they will say or how they will receive what I say. I don't think I have anything to say that will reach them. God, I'm scared. Help me."

At that moment, words came to my mind. Words that I had not recently thought about. They were God's promise to Abraham when the Lord asked him to leave his home and go out into an unknown land. Abraham was cowed by the prospect until the voice of God came to him:

Do not be afraid, Abram.
    I am your shield,
    your very great reward. (Genesis 15:1)

How did those words come to me just then? I hadn't read them in a long time. But that one sentence became the comforting and strengthening voice I needed. I sensed God saying, "Go out there, and I will protect you. I am your shield. And however people may react, your reward will be in knowing that you are mine."

That gave me a measure of courage: God as my great—my "exceeding great"—reward. I did go to the university. I did speak, though I do not remember much of what I said. People may have responded. But I was the one who most needed grace and who received it. I took to heart God's promise: *I am . . . your very great reward.*

As I later reflected back on those days, I began to understand that my emotional paralysis had come in part because I was afraid of losing my identity as a public speaker. My dark time came out of my need to sustain success. Since I was sixteen and had won a countywide speech contest, I had been speaking (and preaching). I loved sports, but I was tall and a bit awkward and didn't get much encouragement. I was also a bit reserved. So as often happens with introverts, in speaking and studies I began to find my own talents and gifts.

As years passed, I had become known as a communicator. But what if that gift was taken away? What if I could not be a speaker, a radio or TV presenter, a preacher in demand? If that was my identity and it was taken away, who was I?

I agree with Parker Palmer that the biggest shadow inside many leaders is deep insecurity about their own identity. We become so "hooked up with external, institutional functions that we may literally die when those functions are taken away from us."[2]

That connects deeply with the inner struggle I was then facing.

In those words to Abram I sensed that incomparable Voice saying, "Leighton, you matter to me not because you are a good speaker or preacher. I made you. I value you. Not for your communication skills but simply because you are my son and I love you for the one I have made you to be."

These thoughts penetrated to my core. I was able to get through the week in Tulsa without my part being a total shambles. Although it was many weeks before the darkness totally lifted, the echo of the reassuring voice continued to be a source of strength.

As I related this incident to a young colleague, he reminded me how Jesus challenged his first disciples right at the point of their "core competency"—fishing (see Luke 5)! As Luke recounts, Jesus called to Peter and his fellow fishermen from the shore early one morning and asked if he could use their boat to speak to the crowds. Then he told Peter, "Put out into deep water and let your nets down for a catch."

Peter was skeptical. "We've worked hard all night and haven't caught anything," he said. "But because you say so, I will let down the nets."

They caught so many their nets were about to break. Peter was so astonished that he went to his knees and said, "Go away from me, Lord; I am a sinful man."

Jesus responded, "Don't be afraid; from now on you will fish for people."

That first call to them came as a challenge. If they were to work for his kingdom, they couldn't do it on their own. It was not all about them.

———

There are times when it *is* about us. A few years after that miserable flight home from Seattle, I hit another pocket of inner turbulence. This was a Jacob-like dark night.

In the biblical story, Jacob is a devious and cheating man. He runs away from his dysfunctional family to another country. On the way, as he sleeps in the desert he has a dream of angels descending and ascending a ladder reaching to heaven, and God is standing close and promising him a future beyond his own grasping schemes.

In his new country Jacob found a wife he deeply loved. But when he finally headed back home he had to face his inner demons and the brother whose birthright he stole years before.

Jacob sent his family ahead. Then, alone, he sat at night by the river Jabbok, dreading how Esau would confront him. He was terribly afraid. But Jacob learned that what he should fear is the enemy within, the shadow in his own soul.

That night the figure of a man appeared and wrestled with Jacob through the night (see Genesis 32). As day broke, he wrenched Jacob's hip socket and was ready to call off the match.

"Let me go," he said, "it is almost day."

But Jacob refused. Aware at last of the monster deep down he said, "I will not let you go unless you bless me."

The strange wrestler asked Jacob's name. Then he told him, "Your name will no longer be Jacob, but Israel, because you have struggled with God and with man and have overcome."

How significant that change was, a changed name for a changed person. Jacob is now Israel—a "struggler with God." Pressed by God down to the ground, he is, as it were, an archetype. His story speaks to all of us who go through that downward and inward journey. He helps us to hear the incomparable Voice that names us and grounds us in the reality of what God has made us to be.

Jacob had to face the fault lines that divided Jacob from Israel.

I needed to let the rumblings from my inner earthquakes bring my needs to the surface. The need to control. To be competent. To find love at whatever cost.

Our family was spending a week in March on the east coast of Florida for a spring break. Our daughter Debbie joined us from college; Sandy was recovering from serious heart fibrillation followed by surgery; Kevin was almost a teenager with the challenges those years bring. Our familiar family patterns were changing. The last year had been trying. We needed time together.

But while the family was at the condo, I walked alone to the beach, peering blankly at a gray-pleated ocean, under a vast and endless March sky. I felt the chill of both inside. Locked into a vault of my own emotions, I wasn't much fun to be around.

Some hours earlier Jeanie asked me a troubling question, which pierced me like a poker jabbed into a fire. She had come across something I had written that surprised and hurt her deeply. It led to a painful conversation, which made us aware that as much as we loved each other, we had been so caught up in the roles we were living out—mom and dad, traveling preacher, homemaker— that we were out of touch with each other's deepest needs.

I had hurt Jeanie and I was distressed. Her brother Billy had said, "Leighton is a man with no guile." I suppose he meant I didn't keep things hidden. But I had disappointed myself and Jeanie. I was not as guileless as I liked to think I was.

A sense of futility, an inability to get beyond my own emotions to touch the rest of the family, and a mix of self-pity and helplessness wrapped around me like a chilly shroud. I needed to get away for a bit, for their sake and mine.

Instead of Florida sunshine, a dimness descended on that beach. Why?

Part of that pain came from deep loneliness, not just that of a public figure but that "long loneliness" Dorothy Day wrote about which resides in the deepest places of our hearts. It cannot be satisfied with surface achievements. For me that longing within was rooted in my two mothers—one who, as I will explain later, let me go, and one who would not. The longing to be loved was a kind of two-edged sword, creating both a desire to be held close and to be set free. It could have led me in the wrong direction. And in holding that longing for love and affirmation inside, I had hurt Jeanie and distanced myself from her.

So I had walked alone to the beach. The night was lovely, star-bright. But the universe felt as cold and unyielding as my heart.

I shivered. Tried to form a prayer. But I had no words clear enough to voice. Finally, a single word came.

"Love."

I spoke it aloud. To myself? Or God? Then waited.

For what?

No voice came, just the rolling of the waves. But deep inside a door opened. The next day I asked forgiveness from Jeanie for hurting her. I was able to express love freshly and spontaneously to her and the children.

The following night I walked again, alone, to the beach, and lifted another one-word prayer.

"Joy."

That night and in the days that followed I found joy, fun, and laughter with my family. When we returned home Jeanie and I found we were bound together even more deeply.

On the surface, the river of my life was flowing rapidly, sometimes choppy, but with a sense of direction. The outer Leighton Ford had been affirmed: I had become fairly well known. But what about the inner course of the river? The invisible currents moving under the surface?

I was yet to learn the full story of my adoption and the two names given me: Leighton for the adopted son and Peter for the birth son. Were there hidden connections between the two? Between the genes I had been born with and the expectations I had grown up with? What was the thread that tied Leighton and Peter together?

What needed to be known, recognized, accepted as real, surrendered, healed, even embraced?

What was surging and surfacing from deep within? What about the poetic instincts that had been buried? What to do with the sexual desires and longings for deeper intimacy? Was I in touch with the adventurous, risking, untamed parts of myself, and how would I express them? Was I afraid of being clutched by my adoptive mother or, as I would learn, separated from my birth mother? Was there an inborn fear of being detached from those I loved and who loved me? Could I experience and grow from failure? And criticism?

In short, as I stood alone that night on the Florida coast, was God whispering to me—in the "stillness between two waves of the sea" (T. S. Eliot)—of his sure and certain love for me just as I was?[3]

The Inward and Downward Journey

An earthquake is a fitting simile for our own inner turbulence. We know that earthquakes—and tsunamis—come from deep fault lines. The huge tectonic plates that are displaced deep in the earth shift with great force, causing the violent upheavals on the surface.

These shifts can cause great damage. Yet, as the British physicist and theologian John Polkinghorne points out, they also release fresh new life into the ocean and the atmosphere.[4] Between the plates, new material wells up from the inside and replenishes the surface of the earth.

I was sensing an inner fault line. These inner upheavals were surprising, painful. But just as Polkinghorne said, they released new creativity in me.

I had become, I suppose, a somewhat successful, respected evangelist. But there was a voice calling me downward. Showing me that the way of the kingdom is not ascent but descent. From being a featured speaker to seeing a man turned away from my appearance because of his color. Descending from my comfortable seat during a conference to sit on the floor with hippies.

Those years were also down in terms of dealing with a fear of failure. My mother Olive's certainty that I must be "better than" others meant better results, more decisions for Christ. Yet was that the main way to measure a calling?

I knew that people were touched and changed through our work. Yet that quiet voice kept calling and challenging me not to preach or live a life (or a gospel) divided.

I faced a transition, a time to discern my calling anew. And that calling was not just to *do* God's work but to *be* God's person in a deeper way.

Who we are, wrote Thomas Keating, is "the great question of the second half of the spiritual journey."[5] This journey is not a success story but "a series of humiliations of the false self that become more and more profound."

This spiritual journey, he suggested, is like "an archeological dig through the various stages of our lives." As archaeologists uncover the layers of ancient civilizations, so the Holy Spirit, the divine therapist, brings "us to the truth about ourselves."[6] And through this transition God brings us to springtime for our souls. I needed to face the humus of life, the humility of knowing God loved me simply for who I was, not for how I could perform.

p. 11-21

9

PIECES IN THE
IDENTITY PUZZLE

Who are my mother and my brothers?
Whoever does God's will is my brother and sister and mother.

Mark 3:33, 35

In the year 1300, when he was thirty-five and at the threshold of a new journey, the poet Dante Alighieri wrote these words:

Midway this way of life we're bound upon,
I woke to find myself in a dark wood,
Where the right road was wholly lost and gone.[1]

In her study of Dante's great poem, Helen Luke points out that the threshold of a new journey usually arrives at midlife.[2] That was true of many biblical characters. When Abram was well along in years, he was called to a new country; when Jacob fell asleep in the desert, he dreamed of a ladder dropped down from heaven; when Moses stopped to gaze at a burning bush, his life was

....
93

changed; when Paul was arrested by a vision of the risen Jesus on the road to Damascus, his eyes were opened. Many of these biblical characters received a new name that symbolized their new calling.

Dante had his own journey. It led through a dark wood and after many twists and turns came to its end. His journey is titled the *Divine Comedy* not because it was funny but because it was a happy one. The story he wrote goes back nearly nine centuries but still speaks powerfully today.

I was also at the midpoint of my life when I woke to a larger sense of my identity and deeper understanding of my calling. For me that new waking was not in a dark wood but in a busy corridor at O'Hare Airport in Chicago.

I had known since age twelve that I was adopted. But until my late forties I gave little thought to how it came about. Then, watching *Roots*, a television series about African Americans discovering their ancestry, I began to wonder: Could my biological parents still be alive? What about my birth heritage?

So in the spring of 1980 I flew to Chicago for a ministry meeting. My more compelling reason for going, however, was to find out more about who I was and where I came from.

I had enlisted the help of a good friend in Canada, and he was coming to meet me with what he had found. I remember standing outside the O'Hare restaurant oblivious to the crowds rushing by and staring at the official-looking document he handed to me.

Dated June 26, 1933, it read:

In the matter of PETER MORGAN MAHAFFY registered under the Vital Statistics Acts without any Christian name . . .

Charles Richard Ford, and his wife Etta Olive Ford are hereby authorized to adopt the said Peter Morgan Mahaffy . . . to be known hereafter as Leighton Frederick Sandys Ford.

I paused and tried to digest it. Until now I had only the most minimal information about my family of origin.

Who were the Mahaffys? Why Peter? Why Morgan? Who chose those names? Why had it taken more than a year and a half after my birth to have the adoption officially registered?

Studying the birth certificate I mused: Was I *Leighton Frederick Sandys Ford* or *Peter Morgan Mahaffy*? Or both?

All I knew at this point is that I now had more names: Leighton Frederick Sandys . . . Peter Morgan . . . Mahaffy . . . Ford.

This was the end of a short search and the start of a much longer one. Who was I with these many names?

———

That day brought clues to my family of origin.

I had accepted being adopted with little questioning and, unlike some adopted children, with no resentment, or burning curiosity to know more about my family of origin. I had felt loved and chosen, even special.

But watching *Roots* triggered a question: Could my biological parents still be living? If so, how would I find them if I wanted to? What heritage might I have that might be interesting? Here I was asking in a whole new way: who was I—this *Leighton Peter Ford?*

In one sense I knew very well who I was: son, husband, father, preacher.

As Thomas Keating wrote, in our life journey we spend the first part of our lives finding a role—professional or parent, executive or explorer, solder or artist. But "the paradox is that we can never fully fulfill our role until we are ready to let it go."[3]

Was I to let go of the roles I had played for nearly fifty years? Was I to take on a whole new persona or practice? Or were my Leighton and Peter names to be integrated in a whole new way?

In my own journey I had been listening to many voices those first forty-nine years.

There had been *formative voices* like those of my adoptive mother Olive, my brother-in-law Billy, and the voice of my wife, Jeanie.

There had been *disturbing* voices, some of an inner longing and some from the tumultuous world around.

There had been a time of *muted voice*, an in-between time when I had been pondering a new calling for my life and work.

Now it was time to ask, Through what other voices has my name been called? How would these previously unknown threads be woven into the pattern of my life and calling?

As the poet Christian Wiman writes, "To be innocent is to retain that space in your heart that once heard a still, small voice saying not so much your name as your nature."[4]

Isn't this the large question of life for each of us? Who am I? And who am I to become? And, most of all, who do I belong to? As the title of a painting by Paul Gauguin asks: *Where Do We Come From? What Are We? Where Are We Going?*

It is a question to ask early in our formative years. To ask at midpoint, as I did at O'Hare. To ask without ceasing right to the end of life. And surely, to ask when finally we come into God's presence.

"I am here. Do you know me?"

And the answer we hope to hear then: "I know you. Welcome."

———

On a cold January day in the winter of 1931, in Kingston, Ontario, Tom and Dorothy made love.

He was a tall, handsome engineering student at Queens University, she the pretty, sixteen-year-old daughter of a Presbyterian minister. They had met the summer before at Orchard Point Inn, a resort on Lake Simcoe, where Dorothy was on the summer staff.

Smitten by him, she wrote in her journal of meeting a charming young man, hoping this summer lakeside romance would be more than another "case."

Their case was not entirely a passing summer fancy. It lasted through the end of that year when they were both back in Kingston.

Their lovemaking had its effect.

Nine months later, in October, I was the result.

———

Although our deepest identity is grounded in Christ as God's beloved, we spend our lives trying to assemble the pieces of our family history into an image we can see and understand. Who am I? Who has brought me into the world, and what do we have in common or not?

These questions underlie our search for living into the person we were created to become. As we seek to move forward in growth and calling, we look back in hopes of understanding what has brought us to the next threshold in our lives. What clues or insights might help us anticipate and shape what lies ahead?

The dark nights of my own emotional and spiritual struggles made such questions more urgent than ever. Drawn by my own questions of identity, I went in search of my birth parents. So it was that in 1980, a few days after my forty-ninth birthday, I drove north from Toronto to Orillia, Ontario, to meet my birth mother, Dorothy, for the first time.

As I drove north I recalled the many summers, years before, that I had passed through this small city on the way to the Muskoka Lakes.

I had also preached at a series of meetings there in 1956, never dreaming that my birth mother was living just a few blocks away from the lakeside hotel where Jeanie and I stayed for two weeks.

I thought back to that day a few months before in O'Hare Airport when I first read about Peter Morgan Mahaffy, registered without any Christian name, then to be known as Leighton Frederick Sandys Ford.

Based on this new information, a friend had volunteered to help me search for my birth parents. My adoptive mother had told me my father was named Harris, and that my mother was the daughter of an Anglican bishop. We found no Anglican bishop named Mahaffy but did learn that the daughter of a Presbyterian minister named F. W. Mahaffy lived in Orillia. My friend called several times to say he had some news for her, but she was not willing to talk to a stranger. Finally, he decided he needed to show up at her house, so he drove to this small city north of Toronto in a snowstorm, knocked at her door, and introduced himself.

"Well," she said, "you're persistent. You better come in."

Over a cup of tea, he said, "I do have news for you. Good news. A friend of mine is looking for his birth mother."

She looked dubious and asked what year his friend was born.

"Nineteen thirty-one."

"What month?"

"October."

"October 22?" she asked.

"Yes."

Hours later he called. He had met my mother. Her name was Dorothy. She lived alone, although she had three other sons. She was willing to talk to me.

So now I was on the way to meet her, full of questions and wondering what she would be like.

As I pulled up to her one-story house, she was waiting out front by a lone pine tree, wearing open-toed sandals with a toe on one foot splayed out and another turned under. She was five-foot-four, a bit stout, and wore a fuzzy, rose-colored cardigan with one button fastened.

I got out of the car, and we looked at each other a moment. She smiled. I said, "My mother" and went and gave her a hug, and we went inside.

While she fixed tea and a Chelsea bun, I looked around her cluttered kitchen. On a chest of drawers were two dozen books, a card and photo from me, and a songbook she had somehow found from my preaching series twenty-four years before.

"I'm very nervous," she said as she bustled around. We talked a bit about squirrels she heard in the attic, problems with the roof, other things that made her anxious.

How, she wondered, had I found her after so long? I explained about watching *Roots*. "Your roots are Toronto," she said. "You were born at Toronto Western Hospital."

"I thought of you every year. When October came I usually got depressed. I wondered if every tall young man I passed on the street might be my son." She showed me photos of herself at twenty-one (she was very pretty) and of her family. She said I looked like her father.

Dorothy told me that when she became pregnant her mother arranged for her to live in Toronto until I was born. The adoption was handled privately. My adoptive mother-to-be, Olive, had somehow checked out her family before the adoption, perhaps had even visited her father's church in Kingston.

On her bedroom floor I noticed a single white candle in a pool of wax.

"What's the white candle for?" I asked.

"Purity," she said, "I have never told anybody. I burn that candle for purity." Then she added, "My father never said a word to me about my having a child."

"Why not?"

"How could he? A minister. And we lived in a small town."

I realized that I was conceived in love, even if unwisely. It was a love that cost her deeply. That candle on the floor may have been burning for purity—but also for a long loneliness that eventually took her to live and die near the lake of her first love.

"What about my name—Peter? You asked when I first called if I knew why I was named Peter and said it was a code."

"Haven't you read about Peter in the Bible?" She found her King James Bible, stuffed with notes, and looked up the place about Peter denying Jesus.

"Is that the code? That Peter denied Jesus and came back?"

"Nothing about you," she said. "About your father." I was "Peter" it seems because my father had denied me (and her), and yet I could be a beloved son.

"I just wanted you to have a good home with two parents since Tom wouldn't marry me. Oh . . . I let that name slip."

"Tom?" I said, "Was he a Harris?"

"Yes. An engineering student at Queens. Tall, with red hair and green eyes. And he tripped and fell the first time he came to see me."

She met him at a summer resort where she worked as a waitress. The next winter, some place in that university town, they came together.

"I was too affectionate," was all she said.

She later married a brilliant and hard-drinking Irish-Canadian doctor and had three more sons. They lived in a northern Ontario mining town until she and her husband separated. She eventually moved to Orillia.

When it was time to leave I put my arms around her and said a prayer. I would be back, I told her. I added, "What can I do for you?"

She had two words. "Love me."

I was able to bring some love into Dorothy's life, but I also brought her renewed pain. When she carried me through nine pregnant months she was carrying that pain. To give me away, to remember me always on my birthday, to wonder if I was that tall young man on the street, all must have brought recurring pangs. When I suddenly came into her life fifty years later the emotional upheaval was powerful.

Across the years I visited with her many times. Connecting was not always easy. When I phoned, Dorothy usually had to do something first—perhaps turn off the kettle—before she could talk. Once I could not reach her for weeks. She had been hospitalized because of an emotional collapse. Small wonder that when I called it usually took her moments, even minutes, to gather herself enough to talk.

During one visit she had said, "Leighton, you can talk all you want about Jesus, but when you don't have someone to sit with, talk with, have a cup of tea with on a cold winter night, it's very hard." All I could do then was to kneel and put my arms around her.

What Did I Hear from These Two Voices?

Both mothers—my birth mother and my adoptive mother—offered me love in their own way. I owe much to both. To Dorothy for giving me birth. To Olive for adopting me into her home, introducing me to faith, and guiding me into the man I have become.

And yet I realize that having one mother who let me go and one who would not has left its imprint, the fear of being abandoned and a resistance to being controlled.

Those two opposite tendencies, reacting against a smothering love and anxious about a relinquishing love, could have been destructive. Instead, this tension has been more creative and less toxic than it might have been. It's a testimony to how the grace-full voice of God can transform those imperfect voices that surround us and transpose the discords into his song of grace.

Having two mothers who were so lonely and had to survive very much on their own has given me a strong commitment to encourage and support women in ministry. It has also taught me that I cannot be a rescuer in unhealthy ways of those who carry deep wounds from life. To discern the difference calls for a lifetime of listening.

In this time of uncovering the roots of my life, I heard the voice of love even more clearly.

The Sound of Bells

On a Sunday afternoon seventeen years after our first meeting, I again pulled to a stop in front of the one-story brick house where I met Dorothy the first time.

Four days ago a handyman had found her on the floor, apparently dead for several days, from an internal hemorrhage.

I sat for a while, thinking. Remembering.

At last I walked from my car up the front walk to her house. It was 7:00 p.m. At that exact moment church bells began to ring out an old gospel song:

Softly and tenderly Jesus is calling

Calling to you and to me . . .

Come home, come home,

You who are weary, come home.[5]

Later that evening I read from a large, shiny black journal Dorothy had kept and had shown me on my first visit. I came to an entry made at that lake resort only a few miles away.

The summer has come and gone. From July 4—August 19 I was at the Orchard Point Inn Atherley, Ont. Met a very charming young man there. Not quite sure whether my liking for him is transitory or otherwise. Rather hope it is not just another "case."

This charming young man was my father, Tom. The journal abruptly broke off in the spring of 1931. After a long gap came a cryptic note:

June 17, 1932—Monday
Much water has flowed under the bridge since last entry in here. Many things—important and trivial have come to pass. But much must remain unrecorded. Be it sufficient that all has turned out well and let us hope for the best.

Nearly two years later she wrote:

Have finally, I believe, recovered from Tom.

I put the journal down and thought of her life. Of her father the minister who never spoke of her first child. Her lonely marriage. The three sons who lived away. The one son she met so late. The lonely years in the house where she died, also alone.

A small group gathered for her funeral service. Dorothy had requested the reading of a hymn, "O Love That Wilt Not Let Me Go."

When it was time for a few words I said, "This is a home-going for Dorothy. But also a homecoming for me . . . to meet some of you for the first time." I spoke of her longings, of the dark times in her life, as well as the delights she took in books and nature, of all of us needing home.

Knowing her made me even more aware of that "inner voice of love," of the great eternal Lover calling through two mothers, Dorothy, in whom was planted the seed of my life, and, Olive, who planted in me the seed of faith.

Then I told how the bells rang out as I went up the walk to Dorothy's house:

Softly and tenderly
Jesus is calling . . .
Come home.

Afterward, the local Presbyterian minister told me he was perplexed.

"Those bells had to be from our church. We are the only one in the city that has chimes. But I don't understand why they went off at 7 p.m. They're set to chime at noon and at five. I must ask the caretaker about it."

Later my half-brother Bob took me aside. "I can't get over those bells ringing when they did," he said. The song played by the bells had stirred a connection that he needed to share. "I need to tell you something. Do you know why Mother moved here?"

After the separation from his father, he told me, Dorothy had come to Orillia and arranged for her house to be built. The next year she moved here with her sons.

"She moved here because she wanted to reconnect with the love of her life. That liaison with Tom was probably the happiest time of her life. And also the most devastating."

A few miles from here, in a long ago summer, Dorothy met a charming man. He had let her go. So had her father. And so had her husband.

She had moved to a place where she could remember one charming, enchanting summer and be close to the great love of her life, never dreaming she would again hold the child of that love.

Small wonder that on her headstone the words she requested were the same ones she selected from the hymn for her funeral: "O love that will'st not let me go."

I think again of the song of the bells:

Come home,
Come home.

I hope she heard the bells ring.

—∿∿—

Three years after meeting my biological mother, Dorothy, I waited at a shopping center in Charlotte, North Carolina, to meet Tom, my biological father.

A few weeks before, a friend delivered a letter from me to Tom at his winter home in Sarasota, Florida. I had thought carefully about how to contact him. I hardly wanted to show up without warning to announce myself as his son from a long ago romance. So I had written, telling him about my meeting with Dorothy, and asking if we could meet.

"Message delivered," my friend told me on the phone. "But I don't think you're likely to hear from him."

He guessed wrong. Tom shared my letter with his wife, Dot, who knew that before their marriage he had fathered a son with another woman. Dot urged him to call his lawyer brother, who had helped to arrange my adoption, to ask if he had heard of me.

"Sure," John said. "He's a well-known preacher. I think some of our family have heard him speak. Why?"

"He's my son!" said Tom.

A few weeks later while I was away in Australia, Jeanie called to say Tom had written me a letter. She read it to me over the phone.

"It was quite a shock to me to be presented with the actual fact that I am the father of a fifty-year-old son of your prominence," he wrote. "I am not a religious or church-going person. Most of my career has been in sales or executive positions with a great deal of entertaining and substantial drinking." He made clear he had no interest in discussing religion.

When I returned home I called him and he agreed to meet on his way back to Ontario from Florida.

So I parked in that shopping center, waiting, and wondering. Would I look like him? What would I learn from him about my own background? What would we talk about?

The only clue my mother Olive had given me was that my father was a Harris, and she hinted that he was from a fairly prominent family. My birth mother, Dorothy, had told me he studied engineering at university.

Their car pulled up, and Tom got out. We shook hands, sizing each other up.

He was imposing. A big man, much taller than my six foot four inches, and much heavier. He had huge hands, a shock of white hair, bright blue eyes, and a foot that dropped down from some nerve injury.

I turned to his wife, Dot. "Thanks for coming! Jeanie wants to meet you. We can't wait to get acquainted."

At our home we chatted over glasses of iced tea. Dot was friendly and outgoing, Tom quiet-spoken. He smoked as we talked. Then the phone rang. It was Jeanie's brother Billy, calling unexpectedly. When I told him my birth father had just arrived, Billy asked to speak to him. Tom came back a few minutes later, puffing on a cigarette, and shaking his head.

"Whew. I just talked to Billy Graham!"

We learned a lot that day about family heritage. My paternal grandmother, Anna Louise, was not Canadian born. Her father,

Bill Monroe, left Ontario to fight as a mercenary in the American Civil War. In Arkansas he became an aide to a colonel who was fatally wounded at the battle of Pea Ridge.

Monroe took the news of his death and a valuable hunting watch to the colonel's wife, fell in love with the widow's daughter Dora, and they married. He bought a cotton farm; they had three children.

When he and Dora both died in a yellow-fever epidemic, relatives took two-year-old Anna Louise back to live with her grandmother in Ontario.

Tom later told me Louise used to listen to me speak on Billy's *Hour of Decision*, never realizing her favorite radio preacher was her grandson!

For years I had kept a photo my adopted mother, Olive, took when I was about ten years old, showing me sitting in an Adirondack chair in front of an impressive two-story house. I had no idea where it was located or why she took the picture.

The house in that mysterious photo, I learned from Tom, was Brucefield, the ancestral house of the Harris family just outside Brantford. One of the first Harrises to come to Ontario was a farmer known as "Elder John" for his horseback preaching rides through the countryside. To devote more time to preaching he began to invent more efficient farm machinery. His son Alanson turned this into a family venture that grew into Massey-Harris (later Massey-Ferguson) one of the most successful international farm implement companies.

The Harris descendants came to play a distinguished place in Canadian life. Alanson was a lay evangelist as well as a businessman. The Baptist leader Elmore Harris, a relative, founded a small Bible school that has now become Tyndale University College and Seminary, where I have lectured and taught several times. When I spoke at one Tyndale graduation ceremony, our daughter, Debbie, was with me. I told her, "This school was started by your great-great-great-grandfather's brother!"

Another cousin, Lawren Harris, is widely regarded as the most eminent Canadian artist of the past century, a founder of the influential Group of Seven, a band of artists known for establishing an innovative school of Canadian landscape painting.

Across generations the Baptist faith of the early Harris settlers faded away. Tom's father was not a churchgoer. Lawren Harris promoted the semi-religious thought known as Theosophy. Tom's other son, my late half-brother Morgan, was a practicing Zen Buddhist. So my two families—one by birth, the other by adoption—reflected the changing spiritual landscape of Canada.

Farming. Invention. Entrepreneurship. Preaching. Evangelism. Artistry. Christianity. Other religions. All were in my genes and blood and history.

When I add all these strands together I have to ask: Is the weaving of this thread accidental? Or providential?

Bloodlines and a New Creation

When our stories begin, they are part of a story that started long before we were born. They are stored in our genes, our family history, in the talents and gifts, the strengths and the weaknesses that have been passed on to us.

As Richard Rohr writes, "I'm still carrying my grandfather's genes and my mother's unlived life and my grandmother's sorrow and my grandfather's pain."[6]

What are we to make of such a legacy? How can we consider the mingling of bloodlines and circumstance, of nature and nurture?

Genealogy is very important in the Bible. Look at the long lists of names in Genesis or the Chronicles and the "book of the genealogy of Jesus Christ," with which Matthew begins his Gospel. God's hand was at work through the generations.

When we are joined to Christ we also are part of a new creation. No longer are blood ties paramount, but rather we become new "creatures in Christ Jesus." Grace, as the old theologians taught, does not destroy or discard the old but in a divine alchemy changes and transforms. Grace takes us as we are and grafts us into a new family.

Perhaps God in his sovereign wisdom has placed within each of us an inborn code waiting to emerge. Think of that mysterious hint in the book of Revelation of a "white stone" and a "new name written" which no one knows except the one who receives it (Revelation 2:17). The God who creates this code also is shaping us uniquely so that Christ will be heard in our voices and seen through our faces.

Nevertheless, the old bloodlines matter, and in my case they were passed on from the previous generations through my birth mother, Dorothy, and my birth father, Tom.

I am grateful to them for giving me life, unplanned as that was. Do I wish I had grown up with them as my parents? Not really. Life would have been different. Tom's values were largely secular. Doubtless he and Dorothy would not have given me the exposure to faith that I received from Olive and indirectly from Charles. Yet I liked and admired Tom and would like to have known both him and Dorothy better.

The day after Tom died I wrote these words, part of a longer poem:

My father is dead.
Tom Harris died yesterday morning, quietly
in his home.
He was eighty-six.
Someone asked how I felt.
I just wished I had known him.

. . . .

Will I see him again?
He, I feel confident, would say no
but he never said.
And I, what do I think?
I don't know.
God does.
Our last visit in a small town hospital
on the day before my 65th birthday,
lasted forty minutes.
He, big and failing, lay back on a lounger
in a crowded hall
oxygen going in his nose
awake but weak
words slower, fewer even than
his normal pace.
There was no privacy,
nurses flustering,
an old man nearby demanding
we listen to him.
No time or place to ask those unasked

questions then.
It was what I had expected
not what I had half hoped.
And, would it have made any difference?
I don't know.
I'm glad I met him
I wish I'd known him.
God, can't we have a second chance?

ꙮ10ꙮ

LOSING A SON,
RESTORING A SOUL

Unless a grain of wheat falls into the earth and dies,
it remains alone.

JOHN 12:24 NASB

On the wall of my bedroom is a color photo of our son, Sandy, posed against some large bushes. He is dressed in a tuxedo, starched white shirt, and black bow tie, dressed for his sister's May wedding. His smile is engaging.

Six months and three days later, the celebration has turned to grief.

On the day after Thanksgiving 1981, Jeanie and I are on the way home from Duke Medical Center, where our beloved son has not survived surgery to correct an electrical problem with his heart. Two weeks past his twenty-first birthday, and he is gone. That face in the photo. That engaging smile. Gone. Now, for the years ahead, we will have only his memory.

I look at Jeanie as we make the three-hour drive home. Her face is drawn, gray, sunken. We are silent for a long time. Then, near midnight, she speaks, so softly I can hardly hear what she says: "Well, either there is a God and he is good, or there is no God. It is just as simple as that."

Back home we fall into bed. Hours later our daughter Debbie and our son-in-law Craig also return from Duke. The four of us lie in the king-size bed, huddled in each other's arms, exhausted.

When we wake the next morning to the realization that our lives have changed forever, we are at first numb, unbelieving. And then grief's nuclear reaction sets in. *He is gone. He will not be back. Why had the doctors failed to get Sandy's heart started again after the surgery?*

The first awful grief we felt as all-consuming. I asked a psychiatrist friend, Armand Nicholi, how long it would take to get over Sandy's death. "At least six months," he said. Then he added gently, "As long as it takes."

It's been near forty years, and I still don't know how long it takes. I do remember how that November and first Christmas passed into winter and then into spring. Sometimes, for a moment we would forget and smile and laugh. Then we'd remember Sandy and feel guilty. Sometimes we almost wished the pain would not go away. Without the pain, it felt like we lost our last connection with Sandy.

What helped? Time. Community. Understanding friends. Heartfelt words. And the realization that we had, so to speak, clean grief in the way he died, as clean as grief can be. We had no reason to regret the life he lived, no wasted years or self-inflicted destructive wounds. He had lived his twenty-one years as fully as he could.

But there really is no fix for such grief, is there? No neat way to describe it or deal with it, simply because its edges are ragged. Grief is a stain that spreads its somber colors into the streams of our souls. It becomes not a single moment or event, but a part of the element that runs through all we are.

Grief can at once be the most connecting and most solitary experience of life. Connecting, because we all feel its pain from the earliest loss of a beloved pet to the loss of a playmate who moves away. Solitary, because it shapes itself to the contours of each individual soul.

In many ways Sandy's death drew our little family together. Yet each of us had to come to terms with the loss in our own way. When the doctors told us Sandy had not survived the surgery, Deb said, "I am going to be so angry with God." And she was. For a long time she found herself unable to pray. She felt as if every important man in her life had left her. I had been away in my work so much of her childhood life. Craig was in the first year of his medical residency, working eighty hours a week—often around the clock—and emotionally tired so much of the time. And now, Sandy was gone.

Our sixteen-year-old son Kevin had been away at a weekend camp during Sandy's surgery. When he came home, he was grave and calm. He was a rock of support for Jeanie and me. He soon picked up Sandy's guitar and taught himself to play. Wore one of his brother's shirts. Declared he was going to do everything he wanted to do, and also everything Sandy would have done. He soon found that was impossible.

Jeanie found consolation in some readings, some routine, a few wise friends. But she kept much of her grief deep inside. "The hard thing," I heard her often say, "is getting our faith and our emotions together. I don't understand God's ways, but I do trust his heart."

Jeanie and I were not angry with God. We are not usually angry people, although she was in truth angry with the doctors who had allowed him to continue his distance running after his first heart surgery seven years before. But we did share a deep disappointment at all he could have been in years to come.

Yet with that disappointment, there was also an equally deep sense of gratitude that we had been given the gift of this son, if only for twenty-one years.

At Sandy's memorial service Craig somehow found the strength to sing unaccompanied a lovely contemporary version of words of St. Paul: "For me to live is Christ, to die is gain." He was able to hold his emotions in long enough to get through the song. Then when we stepped into the car to go to the cemetery, he collapsed into tears, sobbing for the new brother he had come to love and had expected to share life with.

That song was true for Sandy. Christ had been the center of his life. And for him to die was gain, life with God forever. But for the rest of us, for Deb and Kevin and Craig, for Jeanie and me, for the friends who adored him and looked up to his leadership, what was the gain? Some were motivated through his death to make life-changing commitments to God. Others walked away from their faith.

Years later at a conference with people of diverse religious backgrounds, I was on a panel moderated by Rabbi Harold Kushner, author of *When Bad Things Happen to Good People*. It was the first time we had met, and until then neither of us realized that we both had lost sons. Kushner asked me, "Leighton, why is it, do you think, that when bad things and tragedies happen, some people survive and are able to recover, while others are so devastated they never get over it. What makes the difference?"

I had never heard that question posed in just that way. I thought for a few moments, realized that no answer could be completely adequate, stepped to the mike and said, "I don't know."

"Neither do I," said Kushner.

Afterward, a woman in the audience came up to me. "You are the first evangelical I have heard say he did not know the answer to something!" she told me. She was a believer herself. We became close friends, and she is now the key leader in our mentoring ministry.

I still do not know the full answer to Kushner's question. I do know that for Jeanie and me and our family, grace was there, strength beyond ourselves to keep trusting, to keep going.

Derailed or Redirected?

I've been asked if I was derailed as a result of this loss. My answer is no. Not derailed. Detoured. In railway terms, on a siding for a while.

Billy Graham, who in so many ways was gracious, was concerned and puzzled at my continuing grief. He asked my friend John, "What's happened to Leighton? Why is it taking him so long to get over Sandy?"

The loss of a beloved person is like an amputation, like losing an arm or a leg. Or in this case, part of my heart. Healing of such a deep loss takes an enormous amount of energy: physically, emotionally, and spiritually.

That is why I have learned to encourage those who have survived a loss not to rush through the aftermath and the pain. In *The*

Attentive Life I wrote about the "paschal mystery." It is the time needed to grieve the old and to prepare to receive the new. This is an absolutely crucial time we must not pass over or rush through.[1]

"Life goes on. It's time to move on." I remember people saying that to us. Their words were well meant but cruel and unhelpful when we were caught in the depths of darkness and grief. Indeed life goes on and should go on, and God will give us what we need. But as the disciples waited forty days between Jesus' death and resurrection and the coming of the Spirit at Pentecost, we must allow time for our spirit to grieve the old, to be prepared to let go and receive the gift of the Spirit we need for our new life.

And whether or not we wished it, life did go on.

Debbie and Kevin had their own grief to deal with. Their young friends did not know how to give them much support. The two of them had to move on with their lives. Jeanie and I gave them extra attention as Deb adjusted to her new marriage and career, and Kevin finished high school.

I had ministry responsibilities. In the months and years ahead I had major speaking engagements in Australia and Canada, which took preparation and energy. Billy had asked me shortly after Sandy's death to chair the program committee for an international conference of evangelists in Amsterdam. I also continued as the chairman and chief fundraiser for the work of the Lausanne Committee for World Evangelization. All of this commanded my attention, and I was glad for the distraction.

Yet in all of this activity, that sense of loss was pressing. I felt as C. S. Lewis did when his new wife Joy Davidman died. "Her absence," he wrote in *A Grief Observed*, "is like the sky, spread over everything."[2]

A year and a half after Sandy's death I was asked to take the lead role at a citywide evangelism effort in our home city of Charlotte. The theme fittingly was "There Is Hope." I was speaking to my own soul as well as to the many thousands who came night after night. My birth father, Tom, and his wife, Dot, were present one night, the first time he had ever heard me speak, and I introduced him to the welcoming applause of the crowd.

On the last weekend of the series, a new member came into our family: Debbie gave birth to our first grandchild, Graham. The man who cut my hair had said to me not long before, "I don't think you will really start to get over Sandy until your first grandchild comes." And he was right. Graham did not fill the empty place. He made his own new place in our family and our hearts.

I was not derailed. I was to be redirected.

Changes

My friend John said that I was markedly different after Sandy, more open, more accessible. If so, how? How did a broken heart change me?

When I preached in the months after Sandy's death people seemed to hear me in a different way. I was not so much a preacher with a cause to promote but more a father with grief to share. I could speak more freely about my own questions and doubts as a pilgrim preacher with the same human struggles as my listeners. People listened more keenly, responded more deeply.

Yet what I said openly grew out of a wound that stayed invisible and inward. It took time, a long time to heal. I do not think it ever healed completely, but we learned how to live with the wound.

Two things I know out of this wounded and healing time. That to love deeply is to hurt deeply. And that out of deep loss we become different people, for better or worse. Suffering breaks us down or breaks us open. For me it brought some valuable gifts at a great cost.

I was less fearful. As Christian in *Pilgrim's Progress* said after he had waded across the surging river, "Brother, I have felt the bottom, and it is sound." My heart was broken. But my faith held, or rather held me.

As I've said earlier, for years I had lived with the fear of not living up to the need to succeed, needing always to be "better than" others, a need instilled in me by my adopted mother. When I failed or let myself down, whether in a spelling contest, a tennis match, or a sermon that did not bring the expected response, I would be deflated. Sandy had carried that same intense desire to do well, even more driven to achieve than I.

His death could have been my ultimate failure, the failure to protect his life. I had failed, as had the doctors, to keep him safe. The rational me knew this was absurd. My emotional self carried a terrible sense of "if only"—*if only we had not gone ahead with the surgery.*

And yet, having crossed that troubled river, it seemed there was nothing more to fear. Including death itself. With that realization came new freedom.

New Places in My Heart

It's been said that there are places in our hearts we don't even know are there until our hearts are broken. When my heart was broken, I found some of those places in my heart. There was more openness to exploring new paths and taking unexpected risks.

Having traveled the world widely, I now wanted to trace the ways of my own heart more deeply.

I would continue in my calling to share the good news, but now I wanted to touch people more personally, not just to speak from a distance.

As we watched our two other wonderful and gifted children, Deb and Kevin, grow into adulthood, I wanted, and needed, other younger men and women in our lives.

It became more important to me to help young leaders run their race for God than to set any records myself.

Writers like the British novelist Susan Howatch and the Catholic priest Henri Nouwen taught me to listen to the inner voice of longing and love instead of the demanding voices around me or the voice of self-preoccupation.

My preaching was more from the heart, but what I sought was not so much more places to preach as more still places to listen.

Silence and solitude, which I had often avoided, became more welcome and compelling.

To be sure, there were also places in my heart where darker thoughts lurked, inclinations that would need to be faced and known. The spiritual journey, strangely enough, may take us from the stance of the older brother to that of the runaway younger one. From the coldness of self-righteousness we move to the warm embrace of a saving grace that rescues us from our foolish ways.

Toward the Second Half of Life

So what was God doing through all of this? To borrow an image from Denise Levertov's poem "The Avowal," I was like a swimmer, buoyed and held by water, face to sky, learning freefall, knowing I was held by an all-surrounding grace not of my own making.

That thread I had followed, frayed as it was, stretched, torn apart, was still there. And I did not let it go. Or, better, it did not let me go.

I do not believe that God brought about Sandy's death to teach me something. I do believe he used it to prepare me and those I loved for what was yet to come. Richard Rohr has written of a spirituality for the second half of life. "The task of the first half," he writes, "is to create a proper *container* for one's life. . . . The task of the second half of life is, quite simply, to find the actual *contents* that this container was meant to hold and deliver."[3]

Here I was, at fifty, asking myself Mary Oliver's question: "What is it you plan to do / with your one wild and precious life?"[4]

The ten years that followed Sandy's death would become a time of leaving and stretching, reaching out to heed fresh voices and new callings.

Debbie began her own career and started a family. Kevin went to university and graduate school.

We moved from the home we had built and lived in for thirty years, with all its treasured memories, to a new one, physically less than a mile away, yet emotionally a great distance.

I would leave Billy's organization and launch a new ministry to identify, develop, and network emerging leaders.

After thirty years I would do a downshift from large crusades and public ministry to a more quiet and hidden one. Some would ask, as a reporter did in a profile in *Christianity Today*, "What's happened to Leighton Ford?"

The time would come, not easily, to step aside from the active leadership of the Lausanne movement and to launch a new initiative to help young leaders to lead to, like, and for Jesus.

On the way home from Duke on that night of loss, my long-time friend and associate Irv Chambers asked whether we might want flowers for Sandy's service. I responded, instinctively, "Let's start a small memorial fund and use whatever comes in to help other young leaders to run their race for the Lord." The Sandy Ford Fund was started within days, the first gift coming from his uncle Billy. In the years since, more than a thousand young men and women around the world have been supported through Sandy's fund in their preparation for ministry.

My book *Sandy: A Heart for God* was a concrete move in this new direction. It was a book I had to write, even though several editors counseled against it. I had already published a half dozen books, mostly about the practice and theology of evangelism. But they were more objective and tutorial. The ideas came from many sources and with quotes from favorite authors.

Sandy came from my heart. It was more than the most personal book I had written. It was written from deep within. I had poured through Sandy's journals, read the hundreds of letters and anecdotes that came from those who knew and loved him. Somehow I was able to step back, read and absorb them, draft the arc of Sandy's life, and with good editorial assistance write his story and mine.

When the final manuscript came from the publisher in a brown paper envelope, I held it and mused: Is this my son's life? Two pounds of paper?

But it was more than another book. It was a heart cry. It was his voice speaking out through my voice. And that is why, even to this day, *Sandy* has had the most impact of anything I have ever written. It was truly written in blood and not just in print. After these many years we still get letters from parents and peers to say how much it has affected them.

Jesus, facing his own death, said that a seed falls into the ground and dies, then multiplies. The fund and the book were the first seed of our new ministry.

So the loss of a son led to the restoring of a soul and a calling.

In Sandy's last note to us, written the night before his surgery, he wrote,

> Whatever happens, I want you to know that I love you both immensely and hopefully the surgery is successful.... The Lord is reminding us of the great love among Christians and purifying us through suffering. It is not easy for me to realize these words even as I write them because I do not know whether my heart will be corrected or that I will wake up to unduly suffer. Thank you for your faithfulness to me and your love. Love, Sandy

I may not always remember the sound of his voice. I will never forget what his heart spoke.

Today I look again at Sandy's photo beside me. I wonder. *What would he look like now, after all these years?* More like himself, his true and mature self, I am sure.

But is that all? Is the beauty of this young man we loved for twenty-one years gone, except as a photo that will fade? I think of words from the Irish poet-philosopher John O'Donohue:

> Beauty is not all brightness. In the shadowlands of pain and despair, we find slow, dark beauty.[5]

⚮11⚭

A MANTLE FALLING,
A SEED GROWING

Behold, I am doing a new thing.

Isaiah 43:19 ESV

I came across the words below in a red journal I found by Sandy's bed a few days after his funeral. I had gone to his room at the Granville West dormitory at the University of North Carolina to gather his belongings and take them home. He had written this summer 1980 journal entry while in France: "I still have dreams of what I would like to do and what life should be. But I am beginning to realize that life to me is really short."

My heart clutched. I had to stop reading. He had no idea how short his life would be.

On his desk I found an unfinished poem *To Dad, for his fiftieth birthday*. He was never able to finish it or give it to me.

What a golden honor it would be to don your mantle,
    to inherit twice times your spirit.
For then you would be me and I would continue to be you.

I wept as I thought of the promise left unfulfilled. I had no way of imagining that his dreams might be realized or that the mantle might fall another way. Nor could I imagine then how Jesus' words about the seed that falls to the ground and bears fruit could come to pass.

"The seed is always buried in the dark earth."[1]

That seed did begin to push its way up, but not quickly. Grief has its own slow and terrible timetable, and grief is tiring. It took all our energy to care for Debbie and Kevin who were dealing with the loss of their brother in their own ways. Jeanie and I somehow kept our ministry and the daily demands of a home going.

The Seed of New Vision

The psychiatrist Karl Menninger used to ask his patients, "Can you stay with the pain?" Pain can become morbid. But it also can become creative. There are places in our heart, it has been said, we do not even know are there until our hearts are broken—broken open. So it was for Jeanie and me. Deep in the pain a seed was growing into the desire to have other younger men and women become part of our lives.

In our very recent "time between dreams" Jeanie and I had agreed to wait for two years before making any changes in my vocational calling. That time was up during the fall Sandy died, and we could not even think about any big changes then. But "the seed is always buried in the dark earth." It was there, though hidden for a while.

My friend Bob Lupton describes the difference between the chaff of the bright idea and the seed of vision. The bright idea is blown away in the busyness and struggle of life; the seed of vision goes deep, deep, deep into the soil of the human heart and pushes up, up, up until it cannot be ignored.

So with us the seed was growing, but slowly, and we could see it first in our own children.

As time passed Debbie's anger and disappointment led to a faith that is real and honest, not facile but one she can share. As I write, I have next to me a letter from her sent years later to a friend, whose own son was dying. She wrote that "anger and frustration at life's cruel jokes" could be "spiritual and godly, a distortion of God's original plan." In her summer mountain home she leads a group of women drawn to her to guide them as they seek a living faith.

For Kevin, the way to discover his own calling and identity came through theological study, personal introspection, a stint in ministry with university students, and a consulting career in which he helps churches find healthy alignments with their mission.

I think back to the part both of them played in a speaking tour Kevin arranged in half a dozen Virginia universities. While I was preparing my presentations, Debbie and I took long walks together at the beach home of friends in California. As we walked, I talked through what I planned to say to these students. She listened, asked clarifying questions, made suggestions, and liked what I planned to present. I felt affirmed by one who mattered to me most.

The days I spent with Kevin on this tour were some of the most memorable of my life. We drove together through Virginia to the various schools, prayed together, shared meals and conversations, and debriefed after each session, sharpening thoughts for the sessions still ahead. Kevin had put together a team of musicians and actors to help in communicating the message. Together we saw God at work in the lives of hundreds of students.

And more seed was yet to bear fruit.

A Closing Way

A Quaker woman was asked how she was able to discern God's way in her life. Her quaint answer: "Way has not often opened before me, but way has often closed behind me."

"Way" was closing for us. We had lost Sandy. And within a few years I would leave Billy's organization.

I continued my preaching and leadership. Then Billy's chairman asked me to meet him. We discussed the changes that would take place as Billy grew older. The chairman proposed that I start my own organization. He was sure I could find support for it.

Jeanie suggested that I talk to Billy in person. I flew to Rochester, Minnesota, where he was having a routine medical checkup. I asked what he thought. "I think you should do what the board says," he responded firmly. He promised that many of his board would support me. "And," he said, "you and I will be closer." That latter part was true. Across the years we did become closer.

I thanked him and flew back to Charlotte, where Jeanie and I agreed it was time for me to exercise my own leadership after thirty years with Billy.

It was intimidating yet exciting to think of starting a new ministry in my fifties.

But it was becoming clear to me that while I would always be an evangelist, my call was in some ways broader than the focus of some of the Graham team. For some of them it may have seemed too broad, so they were concerned I was becoming liberal! If so, I wanted to have a mind fully committed to the truth of God's Word and a heart and vision as open and receptive as Jesus. It also became evident that room would have to be made for Franklin Graham to take over his father's organization in years to come.

So a way was closing, but what was to be the new way? There were many invitations coming to do this or lead that. Should I start a new organization? Or join another? How were we to discern the right way?

A New Way Opens

During those months I was thinking about writing the book about Sandy and his heart for God. A number of editors that I consulted discouraged me. Since Sandy's life was short they suggested it might be better to write about Jeanie and me and our experience of losing a child.

It was practical advice, but not what was in my heart.

One of those editors, Victor Oliver, came to visit me. While we were talking, Kevin came home from high school. Victor asked where he was planning to go for college. Kevin named three schools but said he had not decided. Victor passed on some intriguing advice from the well-known pastor and author A. W. Tozer: "When you have to make a decision, concentrate on loving God from your heart. If there are several doors open, some will likely close. Then if more than one is open, go through the door you want to go, and trust God to make it right."

Based in part on that wise counsel Kevin chose to go to the University of North Carolina at Chapel Hill. But the conversation directed at Kevin also spoke to me. I knew what I *had* to do: write the book on Sandy and trust God to use it even if few read it.

More than writing the book, those words also spoke to Jeanie and me about discernment for the future. Some doors had closed, others were open. Which one would we go through?

On the Way to Australia: the Vision for a New Generation

A few weeks after Sandy's death I had to leave home, very reluctantly, to fly to Australia for an outreach event in Sydney. Halfway across the Pacific, I was musing about the future of the Lausanne movement, which I was serving as chairman. Most of the leaders, I reflected, were getting older. There was a lot of gray hair at our meetings. I wrote in my journal. "Perhaps the next thing for Lausanne is to help raise up the next generation of young leaders." That seed was planted. Later it began to flower in an international conference for emerging leaders held in Singapore in 1987.

On that Australia trip I also became aware of a major leadership shift taking place worldwide. I asked my friend Bishop John Reid who might be the future bishops in Sydney. He thought a moment, then said, "I can think of several blokes in their thirties, but not any in their forties or fifties." Back home I asked other leaders—in government, business, the church—the same question: who are your future leaders? Over and over they cited the thirty-year-olds.

It became clear: a generation of leaders came on the scene after World War II. They were visionaries who started many new ministries. They were now coming into the later years of their leadership. Another generation was emerging, men and women in their thirties with fresh new visions. In between there were lots of managers, but not that many leaders. Who would help to raise up this new generation?

It seemed there was a quiet voice saying: *This is the door; go through it.*

The Voice in a Dream

In fall 1983 I was in Montreal leading a series of citywide gatherings. Jeanie called to say she was coming and had something to tell me. I was surprised but glad I would see her.

She had always tried not to tell me anything she thought might distract me when I was involved in such an intense week. But when she arrived I could tell she was holding something in and could barely wait for a private moment to talk.

"I had a dream," she said, "and it was so real I just had to come and tell you now. I couldn't contain it. In this dream you had left Billy's association and had become part of something else— perhaps World Vision. You were involved in speaking with and helping Christian leaders around the world. It was so real, so convincing, that I couldn't wait to tell you. I just had to come."

Both of us were very moved by what seemed to be guidance from God in a dream. But how this dream might take shape was still not at all clear.

The Voice in a Dialogue

One day during this time of waiting Jeanie asked me to listen to her read from a small book her mother had cherished. It was written by Amy Carmichael, an English woman who served in

India. *His Thoughts Said . . . His Father Said* consists of imaginary dialogues between a son and his Father.

At one point the son asks how he can know it's time to move.

His Father answers, "And it shall be when thou shalt hear a sound of going in the tops of the mulberry trees, that then thou shalt go out to battle." (A reference to a signal God gave to David about when to fight).

"Thou shalt surely hear that sound," says the Father, adding, "There will be a quiet sense of sureness and a sense of peace."

The son is still baffled. It would be easier, he says, if someone else heard the sound too. Or if he could see the sea made into dry land and waters part, as Moses did.

"That may not always be," says the Father. "The sound of going is like the voice of the shepherd that the sheep know, but how they know they could not tell, knowing only to follow."

But the son still wonders what he should do if he does not hear a Voice directing him. And then he comes to this assurance:

> That as he waited, his Father would work and would so shape the events of common life that they would become indications of His will. He was shown also that they would be in accord with some word of Scripture which would be laid upon his heart. This Scripture in the light of these events, and these events in the light of that Scripture, would work together under the hand of his Father, and point in the same direction, and as he followed step by step the way would open before him.[2]

Only, he is warned, his eye must be "single" and his heart not divided.

Those words and others from Bible stories captivated us: David asking for a sign before battle, Moses leading the people through the Red Sea, Jesus promising that his sheep will know his voice.

Like the ancient king, we wanted more than rustling in the treetops as we applied Amy Carmichael's imaginative words to our own uncertainties.

We too had anxious thoughts. But we also had a "quiet sense of sureness and a sense of peace" that God would show the way in his time.

We also could see God "shaping the events of common life." He shaped it in the deepening desire to have other spiritual sons and daughters who would not replace Sandy but could also bring us joy. He shaped it in the changes we could see happening in Billy's organization. We saw it in the approaches made to recruit us from other places.

What, we wondered, would be that "word of Scripture" that would point in the same direction as these events of life?

We read many helpful passages, but none seemed to take hold of our hearts until early June 1985.

The Voice in a Prayer

I was in Oslo chairing a meeting of the international Lausanne Committee. We were trying to decide whether to proceed with a second major Congress on World Evangelization. It was a difficult decision with many challenges and not nearly enough resources of funding and personnel. We came to an impasse, so I suggested we put aside our discussion and spend an hour in prayer, waiting for some sense of leading.

As we knelt quietly together, a young British leader in his prayer quoted these words: "Forget the former things; do not dwell on the past. See, I am doing a new thing! Now it springs up; do you not perceive it?"

Those words from Isaiah seemed to leap into my heart, leaving a deep and powerful impression: This is the word of Scripture we have been looking for, waiting for.

It was as if God was saying,

These past thirty years of crusading around the world have been my call for you. But now is the time to move—not to discard the past but to leave it with gratitude. Now a new thing is springing up: I am raising a new generation of leaders around the world, and your call now is to find them, encourage them, and help them to become my kingdom leaders for the future.

I recognize the danger in taking words of Scripture written hundreds of years before in a totally different context and personalizing them as if they could have been emailed directly to us centuries later. I realize I could make them mean whatever I wanted them to.

But I also believe that Scripture not only *is* the Word of the Lord (for "all Scripture is inspired by God" and is to be read with faith, humility, and obedience), but it also *contains* the Word (in the sense that Scripture must be interpreted wisely in context and in the light of Christ), and also *becomes* the Word of God (as the Spirit uses it to guide our own lives, minds, and hearts).

Those words from Isaiah's time were God's word to Israel in captivity in Babylon, promising a new exodus as God had parted the sea for Moses. They also look forward to the exodus Jesus said he was about to bring to fulfillment at Jerusalem (Luke 9:31). And, as Paul later wrote, what happened to God's people at the first exodus "happened to them to serve as an example, and they were written down to instruct us, on whom the ends of the ages have come" (1 Corinthians 10:11 NRSV).

God's people in all ages have gone through their "times between dreams," whether captivity in Egypt or Babylon, the dark times for Jesus' followers between his passion and death resurrection, the waiting period for the coming of the Spirit at Pentecost, and the testing times of those early Christians and for many believers today.

In these "times between dreams" we are tempted to look back to the past, even to be bound to the past as our security. But God is not so bound. He is always carrying out his liberating work to make his people free. He calls us to wait patiently and then to join with him joyfully in the "new thing" he is doing.

That afternoon in Oslo the decision was made to proceed with the next Lausanne Congress in Manila in 1989. But that day a new ministry was also born in my mind and heart, although it would be months before I would say goodbye officially to the Graham ministry.

A year later in Charlotte we officially launched Leighton Ford Ministries, aiming to identify, develop, and network the emerging leaders for the global cause of Christ. As I made that announcement, Jeanie and my long-time friend and associate Irv Chambers were both by my side. Also there was my beloved father in the faith, Bishop Jack Dain of Australia, who had preceded me as chair of Lausanne. For the years ahead he would be my most important guide and mentor.

Months before, when I showed Sandy's poem about donning my mantle and inheriting my spirit to my friend and colleague Norman Pell, he was moved. "Leighton," he said, "I believe some of Sandy's spirit has been put in you." So often—more often than not—it seems that when the Lord speaks to me it comes through a close friend's words, whether of encouragement or caution.

And this is what I have found. A mantle has fallen—but fallen another way. Instead of my mantle falling on Sandy, his has fallen on me and on many others.

⁂12⁂

THE START OF A SECOND
JOURNEY

Abraham . . . obeyed and went, even though
he did not know where he was going.

HEBREWS 11:8

It's a little after six on an October Sunday morning. I am headed
out for Crowder's Mountain, west of Charlotte, to join a group of
younger leaders who have come for our new Arrow Leadership
program. This morning begins a day of rappelling and rock climbing.

When we planned our two-year leadership program, a number
of experts suggested that it would be good to start with some kind
of outdoor "risk exercise." That way all the younger leaders would be
on equal footing. Reputations and size of ministry wouldn't matter.

As I am about to leave, Jeanie calls sleepily, "You're not going
to try that are you?" I lean over, give her a hug, and say, "I promise
not to do anything foolish."

And I don't intend to. For one thing, I am a bit nervous about heights. And at almost sixty years old I think I can make excuses. It's enough as the leader of "Arrow" to be there and cheer them on but not risk my own life and limbs.

At the top I watch as the first group of young leaders tries on their helmets and climbing equipment. Some look excited. Some are a little green around the gills. The team leader assures everyone that they don't have to go over the top. They just have to climb up, walk to the edge, and then decide whether to try or not. I am glad I don't have to make that decision.

Then I feel a hand on my shoulder. I turn and see Harold, a grizzled outdoorsman and climber who is along as a volunteer guide. He has had a lot of outdoors experience, including Norwegian army Arctic maneuvers.

"Leighton," he says, "You're going to do this. And I'm going to walk you through it."

I freeze. Then nod. How could I not go, when I was the leader? And, truthfully, part of me wants to try something entirely new.

Harold straps on my helmet and vest, and I make my way to the top as the group applauds. I wave back, trying to look totally nonchalant. Inside I feel like a small boy. It's my moment of decision. Will I go or not? As directed, I back up to the very edge. The coach tells me not to look down but straight at him. At his command I lean back, holding tight to my rope, and step over, swerve in a moment of panic, then swing forward and plant my feet on solid rock.

The next few minutes were some of the most exhilarating I have ever experienced. With my long legs, I must have looked like a tall bug banging against the side of the cliff. But as I made my way down, accompanied by the laughter and cheers of the group, I was euphoric. Not only had I overcome my fears and earned my stripes as a leader, but I had experienced a breakthrough, physically, emotionally, even spiritually.

Harold

Harold was, I suppose, a kind of fatherly (or brotherly) coach for me. I never spent time with my father Ford in any kind of outdoor setting. We watched some games together, but he was too reticent to encourage me to go out for sports. My mother Ford was so overprotective that she would never have allowed me to do anything that would involve risk. When I was learning to swim at a summer Bible conference, she would not let me out of her sight. I tried out for my high school football team, and the coach wanted me to stay, but Mom firmly told me no. She was afraid her son might be hurt, and I was, in her view, too sensitive to engage in any kind of rough and tumble. I felt like the proverbial "momma's boy."

So when Harold came up and said, "You're going to go over, and I'm going to walk you through," it was almost as if the voice of the Lord was speaking. For much of my life I had done what others expected. Now it was time to step out, make a decision, take a risk, and launch into a new and unexplored part of my life.

It was as if I had crossed the border into new territory.

That morning at Crowder's (and later taking part in white water rafting and other outdoor ventures) was a kind of signal of how we are always being called onward—called to let go, to reach out, and trust the voice and hand of God to guide and protect. As Harold promised: "I'm going to walk you through it."

Isn't that the story of God's leaders throughout the Bible? Of Abraham called to leave his ancestral home and go into a new land? Of Jacob wrestling with God in the middle of the night, letting go of his old persona and finding a new name? Of Peter and Andrew, James and John, all called to leave everything and follow Jesus into the unknown?

My life journey had been one of letting go and reaching out. Leaving Canada for the United States. Leaving my adoptive family for the Graham clan. Leaving the Graham organization to start a new ministry when I was fifty-four.

That last move was a big risk. It meant leaving the security of a large organization, with guaranteed income and support, to start an entirely new entity without structure, budget, or staff. Yet I had created new structures to carry out activities before—our local Youth for Christ in my teens, a gospel team at college, an evangelistic outreach across Canada, the forming of the new Lausanne Committee. Perhaps, through my birth father, I inherited the genes of a construction engineer.

I had to leave the security of the Graham Association to give free rein to my own call as a leader. And I can also see how starting Leighton Ford Ministries in midlife taught me to understand what young leaders would experience in their own startups.

The Second Journey

British author Susan Howatch writes in some of her novels of the "second journey" in our lives. For me the beginning of that journey was not at all clear. I knew it was the end of a chapter that had taken me preaching around the world for thirty years. But how was the next chapter to unfold?

My second journey involved letting go not just of an organization but also of an identity. I had been known as "Leighton Ford, evangelist, Billy Graham's brother-in-law." People asked, what is Leighton Ford doing now? Even my close associate Irv, who had been joined at hip and heart with me for decades, was wondering where this new venture would take us.

I have always wanted to be an evangelist—sharing the good news and "making friends for God." And at this point I did not stop evangelizing. The years to come would bring some of the most fulfilling and challenging evangelistic opportunities of my ministry—from a university in New Zealand to a concert hall in Sydney to the famous Montreal Forum hockey arena.

But this new calling kept pressing in. In each of these outreach events I invited younger evangelists to join me, to share in the preaching, and to suggest local background for my own messages. We also began a series of evangelism leadership seminars for students preparing for ministry and local church pastors. In each of them a gifted and experienced younger leader served as dean. Though I would be there and be available, they were up front.

Increasingly I was seeing my calling as one to connect and mentor. To identify, develop, and bring together the emerging young evangelists from around the world.

The shape of the ministry was changing. Having been known as a speaker, I was now doing a lot more listening. From addressing large crowds, now I was having up-close and personal "soul conversations" with small groups and individuals. From traveling the world, I was now staying much closer to home.

One afternoon as I sat by a lagoon at Vancouver's Stanley Park, I watched birds take off, circle around, and light again on the surface. I mused, "Hmm, short flights and quick returns. It's time for that."

At its core this calling was not just in the doing but in the becoming. Around this time I came across poet May Sarton's description of her journey:

Now I become myself. It's taken

Time, many years and places;

I have been dissolved and shaken,

Worn other people's faces.[1]

Those words rang true, not as if I were wearing someone else's face, but that as circumstances changed I too was finding a new sense of calling and fulfillment.

As Jesus said to a new follower, "You are Simon. You shall be Peter," I was hearing that inimitable voice calling again, "Leighton ... Peter." That was the thread winding through these changes.

The word *vocation* is related to *vocal*. It means finding the sound of our own voice, discovering and singing the music of our soul.

As I listened more deeply, not only to the voices around but to the inner voice of the Spirit, I found my own voice more fully. I was also enabled to help others to discover their voices so that through them also the voice of Christ would be heard.

This new ministry had two tracks: holding evangelistic events and developing leaders. Like the strands in a Celtic cord, they were woven and belonged together. Yet, with limitations of time and energy, how could we maintain both?

That was the challenge that led into the "second journey."

⚮13⚭

A VOICE AFTER
THE HURRICANE

The voice of the LORD is powerful. . . .
The voice of the LORD breaks the cedars.

PSALM 29:4-5

On September 22, 1989, Hurricane Hugo blasted through Charlotte like a runaway tractor trailer. One of the most savage storms ever to assault the US mainland, it left a trail of deaths and devastation that cost millions of dollars.[1]

As the center of the hurricane passed, Jeanie and I retreated to the center of our house and lay holding each other in the middle of the den on the ground floor, hoping the house would not crash in on us. Again and again we heard the crack-crack-crack of trees being shattered by winds that lashed our city at up to eighty miles per hour.

The next morning we peered out. There was only minor damage to our house. But in our yard we counted twenty-seven trees that had been knocked down. It looked as if a giant wielding a huge ax had lumbered down our street chopping most of the treetops off fifteen feet above the ground.

The doorbell rang. Two out-of-town friends stood on the doorstep, briefcases in hand. They had come to be part of a strategic planning session for our fledgling ministry that was supposed to start that morning. To get to our front door they had to wade through branches, tree limbs, and leaves that covered every square inch of our yard.

We had no lights, no power. It took two weeks before power was fully restored. So we had to abort our planned meeting to strategize about the future and deal with our immediate needs. Where and what would we eat that night? And what help did our neighbors need?

The storm that uprooted us reminded me how frail we humans are when nature howls. As God said to Job, after reminding him of the uncontrollable power of nature, "What do you know?"

Yet it seemed God had his own strategic planning session in mind.

A few days after Hugo I headed to the cottage of some friends at a nearby lake to spend a solitary day of prayer and planning.

That day I spent a long time thinking about the new call I had sensed: to identify and develop the emerging leaders around the world. In my journal I wrote that we wanted "to contribute to a significant advance in the cause of Christ worldwide."

Three years into the new Leighton Ford Ministries we were still running on two tracks—evangelism and leadership development. We were trying to discern our central focus. As it turned out, Hugo helped us to get on the main track, to develop leaders called to the task of evangelism.

I questioned myself that day: What is the vision? What would be a significant advance?

I reviewed the programs we had started and noted some sketchy thoughts about places and times and the need to raise funds. Then I wrote,

> I see that I have started to become a programmer and a fund-raiser. Some of this is needed. But I have lost in the last year some of the heart to invest in people. Jesus *saw* people. Sometimes crowds. Often individuals.
>
> How will we achieve a "significant advance"? Programs and conferences will come and go. People will grow (or diminish) or pass on to others (or not).
>
> The programs and funds are necessary tasks. But I need to start by looking prayerfully until I see the people.

As I waited, it seemed that I heard a quiet voice saying, "If you want to make a difference in the world, it will happen not by multiplying programs but by investing in people."

For some time I had been keeping what I called my GGTW List—Guys and Gals to Watch. These were younger men and women in whom I observed strong potential for leadership. From time to time I would call them, occasionally take one or two along on a ministry trip, and often pray for them.

That day from the list I wrote down a dozen names of younger leaders from around the world I could invest in, and who in turn could mentor others.

Within two years some of them formed the core of our first mentoring group of younger leaders who would meet with me each year. Many of them have since emerged into key positions of leadership in their areas of the world and have also started their own leadership mentoring groups.

Hurricane Hugo interrupted our planning session. But as it shook up our street and our plans, it also opened me to listen in a deep way to "the voice after the storm." It helped us to get on the main track: to help younger leaders to lead more like Jesus and more to him. And to listen more deeply to the voice of his Spirit.

As the Lord said through Isaiah centuries ago:

> As the heavens are higher than the earth,
>> so are my ways higher than your ways
>> and my thoughts than your thoughts.
> As the rain and the snow
>> come down from heaven . . .
> so is my word that goes out from my mouth:
>> It shall not return to me empty,
> but will accomplish what I desire
>> and achieve the purpose for which I sent it.
>> (Isaiah 55:9-11)

Like the rain and snow from heaven, that hurricane gave me a timely reminder: whether it be the forces of nature or the work of God's kingdom, we can make our plans, but we are not ultimately in control. God's ways are better and higher than we can conceive. As a friend once ended a letter to me, "Remember, God really is God, he's not applying for the job."

Vision and Values

The vision after Hugo still needed to be fleshed out. What were the values we wanted to pass on?

Early in our shaping of the new ministry, a leadership-development specialist asked, "Can you put in one sentence what you want to accomplish?" I was stumped for a moment. Then these words came: "Yes, we want to help young leaders to lead more to Jesus and more like Jesus." Later I added and to lead "for Jesus."

I had been writing a book on Jesus as a leader and had been reading and rereading Mark's Gospel, noting the marks of Jesus' leadership. Many Christian leadership books seemed to be largely adapted from secular models. They were helpful, but not singularly based on Jesus' own leadership: the leadership of a son, a storyteller, a servant, and a shepherd-maker.

Our aim would be to center on Jesus. Through the Word and Spirit we would help young leaders worldwide to lead. To lead *to* Jesus (in evangelism), *like* Jesus (in character), and *for* Jesus (in motive.) We began to develop a personalized leadership-development experience that would focus both on the character and competence of ministry leaders. It would lift up a calling to be kingdom seekers and not empire builders, a phrase I have often used in conversations with emerging leaders.

We named this the Arrow Leadership program. That image had come to me when I was speaking at Duke Divinity School chapel and was asked how I had seen Billy Graham change across the years. The picture of an arrow came to mind. "Billy Graham has been like an arrowhead," I suggested, "sharp at the point with the gospel always at the forefront in his preaching. He has also grown broader like an arrowhead at its base as he understands the implications of the gospel for issues like poverty and nuclear weapons. And like the shaft of an arrow growing deeper in the Lord."

The Marks of the Arrow Vision

Not long after Hugo hit, I was in Toronto meeting with the Canadian directors of our new ministry, excitedly sharing with them this fresh vision. They shared my enthusiasm, but then one of them stumped me.

"Tell me," he said, "what *are* these values that you want to pass on?"

I was caught short and was a bit embarrassed. While I had a general notion of what leadership development involved, I had clearly not thought this through. I stammered out a few general thoughts, but the question stayed with me.

The next day Jeanie and I joined a friend for a cruise across Lake Ontario to Niagara Falls. As I lay on the front of his boat, I said a silent prayer, asking the Lord for wisdom and clarity.

Then again came that inner voice. Words came to me, formed in my mind. I sensed they were not just my thoughts. They came through me to my mind, but they also seemed to come from beyond me, words that summed up the values to pass on.

They formed a prayer for emerging leaders who would:

- Have a heart for God
- Love their neighbors and their families
- Lead and serve like Jesus
- Be able to communicate the gospel effectively, with passion, thoughtfulness, creativity, and integrity
- Live humane and holy lives that would make the gospel attractive
- Be aware of their world, alert to their generation
- Act compassionately for the lost and the needy

- Be kingdom seekers, not empire builders
- Long for the unity of God's people
- Learn to pray the work

It was almost as if these words were spoken to me as I rested on the front of the boat. I wrote them down and later added some appropriate Scriptural passages.

Those values in years ahead became the framework for our mentoring and expanded to become the goal and the heart of our leadership ministry. We would aim to develop leaders who would be like arrowheads: sharp in vision, like the point of an arrow; broad in knowledge and wisdom, like its breadth; and deep in spirit, like its shaft.

I repeated this vision often to the men and women who became part of the Arrow program. At their graduation I would go to each one, lay hands of blessing on their head, call them by name, and speak quietly to each one of those phrases:

"Ken, be a kingdom seeker . . ."

"Elizabeth, lead and serve like Jesus . . ."

"Chris, communicate the gospel with creativity and integrity . . ."

"Alison, pray the work . . ."

After the storm, that still voice brought a new focus to our ministry.

On the lake, it brought clarity to our mission.

And then, as if sensing that my hesitant heart might need confirmation, another signal seemed to come.

Late that afternoon, as our boat was returning from Niagara Falls to Toronto, I lay on the front of the boat reflecting on our trip and the insights that had come.

My eyes were drawn to the sky. Above was a cloud, shaped, so it appeared to me, like an arrow, an arrow that intersected what looked like a dove.

Was I seeing things? Hearing things?

Yes, indeed I was.

∂◎14◎∂

WHEN WE LOSE OUR WAY

"David was [in the wilderness] . . . and Jonathan . . .
helped him find strength in God."

1 Samuel 23:15-16

Not too many years ago I got lost in the woods near Linville, a small village high in the North Carolina mountains. For a hundred years people from "low country" have come there to cool off from summer heat and to enjoy fall colors. Linville has a rustic lodge, a hardware store, an old-fashioned family restaurant, four churches, and a golf course. Off the picnic grounds is a path through the woods, and that's where I got lost.

I had been the Sunday speaker for summertime worship at the Wee Kirk and stayed over for a day to relax. Midafternoon my dog, Wrangler, and I went for a walk in the woods. I'd walked there before and thought I knew the path pretty well; it wound a short distance around and back to a small lake.

This time I decided to explore the path further. At a fork I made a mental note of a trail sign posted to guide us on the way back and turned toward what I thought led to the main road. We walked a long way, around a hillside, over a deep stream, winding in different directions, expecting to find where the path led. But with no end in sight, I decided (and Wrangler I think agreed!) we should turn back.

But which way led back? I could locate neither the fork where we had first turned off nor the trail sign. It was getting dark. My mental map was confused by contours of the land, and the angle of the sun didn't help guide us.

It was close to six p.m. I didn't relish the idea of being lost in these woods at night, especially knowing black bears were around. How could I have not gotten a map before setting out? Why had I not told anyone where I was going?

My cell phone was close to powering down, so I realized I better call for help before the charge was totally gone. So I called the nearby Eseeola Lodge hoping I could reach the manager.

"John," I said when he answered, "this is Leighton. I feel foolish but I am really lost in the woods off the picnic grounds. I have no idea where I am and which way to go. Can you help?"

"Where do you think you are?" he asked. "Describe it." I tried to tell him the best I could.

"I think I know where you are," he said, then told me to go another direction. Confused in the woods and hills I had been headed 180 degrees wrong.

"Go for a couple of miles," John said. "It should lead you to Roseboro Road. I'll have one of our security guards meet you there with a pickup and take you back to your car."

"Have him shout out so I can know I am heading in the right direction," I asked.

Relieved, I set off again. Wrangler and I walked for a good forty-five minutes along trails I did not recognize. As evening closed in, every minute seemed longer. I was still unsure I was going the right way, but I trusted that someone who knew the woods had set me right. Then came a final turn and I saw the driver waiting, gave a shout, and he answered back. At last I was "here."

Lines in a poem by David Wagoner take me back vividly to that lost afternoon.

You are surely lost. Stand still. The forest knows
Where you are. You must let it find you.[1]

Finding Myself in a Dark Wood

I wrote earlier about Dante's waking to find (and refinding) himself in a dark wood, where the road was lost and gone.

For me the "lost in a dark wood" times have come at various points. Some I have already described, like the earlier times of deep discouragement and the death of our beloved Sandy.

Others have come when I have made a wrong turn and deliberately gone in a direction I knew was not for the best. Or when I wasn't really paying attention to the deepest longings of my heart. Or when some of our efforts faced impossible roadblocks. Or when someone I thought was a friend spoke untruth to and about me. Or when a member of our family was hurt.

I will never forget flying home from England and going from the airport straight to our daughter Debbie's house. She had a recurrence of breast cancer and was facing months of chemo and radiation. I lay beside her and held her as she sobbed. (It was a bright morning when five years later she got her "all clear" word.)

Another came as I was driving home from a late-night dinner and heard a bump, I jumped out of the car to find I had run over my beloved Australian Cattle Dog, Wrangler. My dog of a lifetime was gone!

One of the darkest came for Jeanie and me at a very crucial time of transition in our ministry. I suddenly found myself questioned and misinterpreted by friends I had long known and trusted. It was a disagreement that could have been prevented. What totally shattered me was an unwillingness to listen and understand.

Behind our house is a schoolyard. In the schoolyard is an iron post that holds a basketball goal. On a cold, black night during this ordeal I walked through that yard trembling with rage and humiliation. I grasped the iron bar with bare hands, shook it, roared into the night and tried to bend and break it.

The despair I felt then was about how I could survive and not let my spirit be broken; I knew I could not make it without the help of friends.

I was lost in the "dark wood" of a wounded soul. Were there voices that would help?

My Anamcharas

"What helped you during that dark time?," asked a young leader who knew something of this situation. And I immediately answered, "My friends, my anamcharas.'"

It is a lovely word, *anamchara*. I love the sound of it. It is the term the ancient Celts used to describe the men and women who were "soul friends" on their life journeys.

It reminds me of that beautiful story of friendship between David and Jonathan, the son of King Saul. Saul, furious with envy at the popularity of his gifted young aide, sought to kill him. David fled and hid in the wilderness. There Jonathan, who loved David as himself, found him and "helped [David] find strength in God" (1 Samuel 23:16).

Before his death Jesus told his followers, "I have called you friends" (John 15:15). After his resurrection he came to two disheartened disciples and opened their eyes to see it was truly him—alive—then and always *the* friend on *their* journey.

He came to me too one miserable night in that ordeal when I was unable to sleep and read these words from Philip Yancey: "Grace means there is nothing we can do to make God love us more.... And grace means there is nothing we can do to make God love us less."[2] Those words girded me with grace.

What a friend we have in Jesus. Yes, and what friends we have in the friends of Jesus. I have relied on these friends in my wilderness times and on my lonely road—friends who believed in and supported me, helped me to find my way again through that dark wood.

What they offered in so many ways will stay with me.

I picture a group of young friends sitting with me by a fire in a mountain home, asking me penetrating questions and then giving me their trust and love.

Helpful perspective came from Jim, a psychologist friend who explained how toxic elements often surface during times of transition. People often project their own desires and fears onto their spiritual leaders. If the leader fails their expectations, they turn on them with as much venom as the adoration they lavished before.

During conflict, he says, there is a cognitive dissonance when values clash and power is at stake. Voices become distorted. Those on all sides dig in and are not willing to listen or find it difficult to listen. Motives are misunderstood, and those involved project onto leaders their own needs. Reason shuts down, and emotions rule. We get wrapped in "the fog of war." The desire for power and control take over. And when those we have trusted let us down, the sense of betrayal is acute.

John, a long-time pastor friend, counseled me by phone. "Leighton, you're too close to the table. Take a step back. You are too close to the situation to see clearly. You need a larger perspective. Back up from the table until you can take a wider view. Remember this is not your whole story."

I told a writer friend how my ability to paint seemed to have deserted me. "Leighton," she said, "those instincts have had to go underground a while to protect some vulnerable parts. Give them time. They will come back."

Needing some time alone to heal and recover, I went off for a few days to a small cabin I rented in a mountain cove. There I journaled and poured out my soul, the hurts, and the wounds in prayer. One night I turned out all the lights, sat on the floor, and with some music in the background began blindly to draw shapes and contours with a marker on a pad. What I drew that night was no ordinary scene. It was a scrim of emotions, scrabbled lines and circles, a pouring out of the anguish within. And somehow it opened inner doors in my psyche and let the dammed up hurt ebb out.

The next morning there was a downpour of mountain rain. The little cabin was hidden and out of sight. So I stripped down, walked out into the downpour, let it pour over me, through my hair, down my body, gather round my feet. And began to feel the confusion and shame wash away.

These and other anamcharas guided me through and out of my dark wood.

Perhaps most of all—next to Jeanie's unfailing trust—there was Jack, the Anglican bishop who was a spiritual father to me. During this painful time, I visited him at his home in the south of England. As we sat in his home, I shared the hurt of what had erupted. He recalled that years before when he was treated unjustly, a wise bishop told him that we can lose by winning and win by losing. And he tenderly said to me, "You just need to find a way to let the pain and hurt go. Hold it loosely even if you can't fix it."

Hold It, Don't Fix It

Soon after this dark period I was speaking at a conference in northern England. I went for a walk one afternoon on a country path through the farm fields. As I came back to the gate to our residence I remembered Jack's words, picked up a stick, and drew a line on the dirt. I stepped across it, and breathed, "Lord, as best I can, I let go of the hurt, the resentment, the anger. I don't know if the breach will ever be repaired. But as much as is in me I leave it behind. Help me to do so."

As the months passed and the hurt began to heal, bitter feelings would rear again. And I could hear Jack's voice saying, "Hold it loosely, Leighton. Don't fix it. Hold it loosely, don't fix it."

Now, many years later, I sense no need to fix it. Rather I am grateful for the insights that often come only through the hardest times.

I will not soon again venture alone, without a map, into deep woods I don't know or without letting someone know where I am going. And I will also seek to remember and pass on lessons I have learned.

Here are a few things I have learned—or am trying to learn:

I have become less naive about people and more aware of how complicated relationships can be. Christian groups can get along well in peacetime, but not so well in conflict.

I have found that my desire to serve and help can make me vulnerable. I have realized my wife's intuitions are more well-tuned than mine.

I tell young leaders to expect conflicts—and that it's important to have written agreements to use mediators when there are intransigent issues.

I can fool myself about motives, my own and others', and only Jesus has totally pure motives.

We need to appreciate those who esteem us, but be wary of those who adore.

When I am wrestling with my own inner changes and challenges and am not able to articulate them, others will sense something going on that makes them anxious. Clear communication matters.

True forgiveness doesn't come easily, but it does set us free.

And I need to remember when someone else does something that raises questions to listen early, trust appropriately, probe gently, and—unless others are sure to be hurt—to leave judgment in God's hands. "To your own master you stand or fall."

What do we do when we lose our way? We can either panic and freeze or stand still and listen for a Voice (and voices) that can tell us where we are and point to where we need to go.

ᔍ15ᔏ

THE VOICE OF BEAUTY

To behold the beauty of the Lord.

<small>Psalm</small> 27:4 KJV

As I write I am looking at one of my earliest watercolors, *Sunset at English Bay*. I'm reliving a memory.

On a July evening in the early 1990s, in Vancouver, Canada, I'm sitting at the window of a condo on the nineteenth floor of a high-rise.

From my window seat I look down at the magnificent Stanley Park, one of the truly spectacular urban parks of the world, almost completely surrounded by water. Its canopy of trees covers miles of hiking trails.

Past a sea wall, the lovely bay stretches toward the far hills of West Vancouver. Three oceangoing vessels rest at anchor, their lights blinking along with the warning lamp at Lighthouse Point.

At sunset the colors captivate me. The many shades of green among the trees, bits of light against the darks. The gray blue evening sky reflected on the waters of the bay. The darker violet of the hills. In the sky a veritable rainbow of blues, scarlet, and a slash of orange is left as the sun sinks below the hills.

This whole month has been a banquet of beauty. During a break from his graduate classes nearby, my son Kevin and I drove for days exploring the interior of British Columbia and on into Alberta's Rocky Mountains. We stopped again and again to marvel at the towering peaks, to walk trails fragrant with conifers, to pick our way onto the cold, blue-green, glacial ice at the base of the mountains.

All the photos we took were later lost. Yet our once-in-a-lifetime trip together, along with the splendor of the natural world, have always stayed with me.

This spot, overlooking English Bay, became for me one of those "thin places" (as the ancient Celts described them), where water and land and sky meet. Here God seems very close.

Both the summer mornings and the sunsets have been times to recognize God's presence in the beauty and order of creation, to see, as an ancient teacher said, "all things in God and God in all things."

The Drawing Power of Beauty

John O'Donohue wrote in *Beauty* that "when we experience beauty we feel called." The Greek word for beauty—*kalos*—is closely related to the verb *kaleō*, which includes the idea of call. "The Beautiful," he writes, "calls us from aloneness into the warmth and wonder of an eternal embrace."[1]

Only later in life have I realized how powerful that call can be.

From my early years I have only a few scattered memories of beauty. In my childhood home there was one lovely painting of a snow scene by a Russian artist. Attractive pieces of jewelry were offered in my parents' store. Maple trees blazed on our streets in a symphony of autumn color.

The surrounding Canadian farmlands of sugar beets and tobacco, although fertile, were flat and drab much of the time. Most buildings, as I remember them, including the churches, tended to be utilitarian rather than awe-inspiring,

It was in the Muskoka Lakes district, where we went often to enjoy a summer Bible conference, that my spirit was touched by the beauty of rocks and water, the greens of the pines, and the deep blues of the lakes. I don't recall that the Bible teachers took pains to point out how "green" the Bible is. They clearly did not have access to the *Green Bible*, where colored highlights show the reality of God's hand in creation on almost every page.

From those summer sessions I do remember this song about experiencing God's love in nature:

Heaven above is softer blue
Earth around is deeper green
Something glows in every hue
Christless eyes have never seen.[2]

Years later my eyes were opened to God's beauty in fresh ways. In the soft hair and warm eyes of my beloved Jeanie. In the loveliness of our children. In exposure to great music and art. Even, occasionally, in some inspired preaching.

Then, in my sixties, I heard another voice of beauty. I discovered that I shared family genes with a famous Canadian artist and that there was an artist waiting in my own soul.

My Own Artist's Way

It was in that same high-rise apartment above English Bay that I was surprised to discover a desire to paint.

One stifling afternoon I was bored with reading. I picked up a book lying in the apartment, *Drawing on the Creative Artist Within*, by Betty Edwards. The author showed the self-portraits of her students the first day of class. They were mostly grotesque. But by the end of the term their work had become beautiful.

How did they learn to do that? The author explained it was all about learning to see from the right side of the brain. I tried one of her exercises involving a photo of Albert Einstein, turned it upside down, drew the shapes I saw, and was amazed. There was a hint of likeness.

When I returned home I took a class called "The Fear of Drawing," and discovered a new avocation: to be a painter. I discovered that artistry is not so much about techniques of painting or poetry as it is finding a new way of seeing.

The discovery was more than about drawing. I also found myself rushing through life without taking the time to see, to really look at a sunset, a tree, a face. Even my own rushed handwriting said, "This scrawl shows a man in a hurry, hard to read." I needed to slow down, to begin to see in a new way, to become more attentive.

Learning to draw and paint took *sight*, asking, What is there? What line? Color? Form? It also took *insight*, asking, What is in there? What is the meaning of what I see?

It made me aware of another voice—the voice of the Artist. Since then, painting has been an important part of my life. The watercolors and pastels I create are a way to express a deep longing for beauty, a way to remember those "thin places," like English Bay at Vancouver, where the sense of God's presence has been very real.

I became aware of inscape—a poetic and artistic sense to see what had been present but not awakened. In times to come it would also help me see God-given gifts in others and help them find what they had not realized.

In our postmodern world people have been treated as numbers, as replaceable parts, as an item on someone's agenda, a program, a screen name. They long to be noticed, to be valued, to have someone pay attention! Not only to be "seen" but to be "inseen"— with insight.[3]

An Artist of the Soul

Isn't that how Jesus saw? As an artist of the soul?

Jesus' artistry was evident in how he saw people—*beyond* their sins, *behind* their behavior, *beneath* their problems—to their hearts. And he reframed them.

Jesus looked at one of his new recruits, a big, brash, raw fisherman and said, "You are Simon, you will be called Cephas [Peter]." With the eyes of an artist he saw not only what Simon was but what he could be.

It was as if he was saying, "Everyone sees and knows Simon the reed. Impetuous. Unstable. I see Peter, the rock man ... on whom I will build my church!"

What if we learned to see not only as gifted artists have seen but even more as Jesus saw!

In Vancouver, years later, I sat outside a church that had once been vital and flourishing, but had grown stagnant and near to closing down. A young friend had been called to be the lead pastor. As we sat in a car talking, he told me how he was second-guessing his call and was filled with misgivings.

"I can't believe they would want me, in my early thirties, to be their pastor. I'm not sure I'm up to it."

I said to him, "Remember God is an artist. He doesn't do copies. He does originals. And if you are called here, God will do something new through you."

And he has. Through the Spirit of God and the gifts of that young man, the dying church is now alive and flourishing.

My word to him that day was also a word to me.

God the artist has continued to do his original work in and through me. Not reproducing the past but opening new vistas. Bringing fresh visions.

Echoes of Jesus

In *The Way It Is*, William Stafford describes "the thread that you follow"—a thread that runs through things that change.[4] That thread has involved paying attention to the various threads or strands that have been woven into my life. These threads, these strands, were so perfectly modeled in Jesus.

When I early sensed the call to preach, that was an echo of Jesus who was the great Storyteller. Mark tells us that Jesus taught many things, but always with a story. Never *without* a story (Mark 4:33). His stories made the kingdom live for his hearers.

Then came my call to be a listening friend and mentor to younger men and women, also an echo of Jesus, the great Friend. "I have called you friends," he said to his followers at their last meal, then laid down his life for them and came alive to be their constant companion.

And the call to be an artist? In that too he is the great model. As Vincent van Gogh said, "Christ is more of an artist than the artists; he works in the living spirit and living flesh; he makes men instead of statues."[5]

So many threads make up the cord of the kingdom of God, the gifts that bind us to God and one another. The sacred story through our stories. Helping each other to see God's vision for us. Offering friendship on the journey. All of these threads and many others are present in Jesus. Each of us can form one of the threads in the cords of his love and grace.

In these autumn years these threads have been woven into my own life and ministry. I have told the story of Jesus across many years and still do.

If I am asked for my mission statement, I now say, "To be an artist of the soul. And a friend on the journey."

16

A VOICE AMONG THE VOICES

A voice came from the cloud.

Luke 9:35

One summer not too long ago, I took my daughter, Debbie, and two of our grown grandchildren to my native Ontario. It was a trip I had wanted to take for a long time to show them places that had been important to me when I was young.

I wanted to remember voices I had heard in those places, voices that were important in shaping my life story.

In Chatham we peered into the windows of the frame house where my mother Ford taught me to pray. In Toronto I walked with my grandson in the park where I learned I was adopted. Heading north through Orillia I showed them St. Andrew's Presbyterian Church, where I preached at one of my first crusades. After a half-hour search, we found the small house where I met my birth mother for the first time.

A highlight of the trip was the two days we spent in Muskoka. The beauty of the place has stayed with me and so have the voices I heard at the Canadian Keswick Bible Conference—where I raised my hand to say I wanted Jesus in my heart, the Bible studies where I learned so much of the great Book, the missionary sessions by the lakeside where we heard of God's work around the world. These were formative.

Clouds Across the Lake

One of my fondest memories is of steamer rides across the lakes. On this recent trip we took a cruise across Lake Muskoka. I was struck by the appearance of a great array of clouds. Stream after brilliant stream of glowing white were a backdrop for the rich blue waters.

Clouds captivate me. I love to watch them. Gaze at them. Paint them. See their changing shapes and formations. Appearing so solid, they are constantly shifting. The darks and lights reflect my own moods. In their movements I sense my own.

But that day those clouds spoke to me beyond their immediate beauty. They touched something deep in my soul.

When the British physicist-theologian John Polkinghorne was asked how, as a scientist, he can believe in answered prayer, he pointed out that there are clock-like happenings in our world, but also areas in life where cloudiness and clearness interlace.[1]

Those borderline areas are the openings where God may be speaking in unpredictable ways: in answered prayer, a brilliant light, a voice speaking out of an overshadowing cloud.

So often clouds appear in Scripture at key moments. When Moses conferred with God on the top of Sinai, there was a thick cloud over the mountain. After a long drought, Elijah the prophet prayed for rain. He waited until his servant saw a cloud "as small as a man's hand" rising from the sea and the sky grew black. Heavy rains came.

The paramount cloud cover came when Jesus took Peter and James and John, led them up a high mountain, and was transfigured. A cloud overshadowed them.

From that cloud came a voice: "This is my Son, whom I love. Listen to him" (Mark 9:7). Out of the clouds God tells us to listen above all and through all to the voice of his Son, his beloved.

An Accumulation of Voices

Remembering those scriptural clouds and watching that huge billowing cloud over Lake Muskoka, I realized how all these voices across my years have been tied together by an "invisible thread"—the quiet and persistent voice of God through Jesus.

God has spoken *in* the clouds and *from* the clouds. But God's voice has so often come to me *like* the clouds: not in a single instant but in an accumulation of voices and happenings.

Accumulation is a fitting word. It makes me think of cumulus clouds, great billows that accumulate a weight of water until finally they let go in a downpour.

Again and again in my life there has been an accumulation—of voices, of events, of passages—that has grown and grown until the rain falls, the sky clears, and clarity comes.

What has been true for me has, I suspect, been so for many of us: a sense of direction coming through many voices, many clouds—waitings, testings, questionings, learnings—until that one clear incomparable Voice is heard.

Isn't that what we see again and again in the Bible? Real people in a real physical world and real time suddenly intersected in a way they could not have predicted, seeing a light and hearing a voice they never encountered before.

The ordinariness of nature is what usually happens. The extraordinary is what God sometimes brings to pass. If we pay attention we may hear God's voice in both, the ordinary and the unexpected.

It is also a reminder that our stories—the stories with the small s—are part of God's Story, the story with the big S.

When God calls our name, he is calling us not only to find our personal identity, to be who we are created to be, but also to enter into his great enterprise of bringing all things together in Christ. To play our part in healing one small part of the great wound in the heart of a bleeding world.

Listening to God and to Others

I think back to some of the stories I have told in this book. I realize that direction from God the Father, the Son, and the Holy Spirit comes over and over through many voices until that one incomparable Voice becomes clear.

How do I know it is God directing me, not just my own thoughts? Or the suggestions of others? I didn't hear a voice out loud telling me it was wrong that Enoch Fears was barred from the Alabama church. Or that I should go and find the hippies thrown out of that meeting in Minneapolis. Were those nudges from God?

When I think back to the stories of Elijah and Peter, I realize that the voice they heard—telling Elijah to keep on prophesying, directing Peter to go and tell the gospel to the house of Cornelius, the Roman centurion—did not come in the midst of turmoil. It came to Elijah after his sojourn in the desert and to Peter during an afternoon nap. In neither case were they seeking to hear something. The voice was unexpected, and it came during a time of confusion when neither knew quite what to do.

And it came as a kind of inner dialogue.

"What are you doing here?" God asked Elijah. "Get up; kill and eat," the Lord said to Peter, who had protested he would not eat "unclean" food. "What God has made clean, you must not call profane."

In times of confusion and turmoil we need to find time to rest, to reflect, to listen to the questions that press into our minds and hearts.

We need to listen humbly—knowing that we may be mistaken.

We need to listen expectantly—trusting that God will show us his way in his time—and in his way.

And we need to listen ready to obey and act, as Elijah and Peter did.

Jesus, the living Word, speaks through the Bible, read and preached. Sometimes this may be through a single sentence. But I can twist isolated texts to fit my plans. So I need to read the Bible as a whole, paying attention to the whole story of what God is doing—creating a world, choosing a people, re-creating a world gone wrong.

For John Calvin the Bible was like a pair of spectacles through which we can see more clearly what God is doing in the world. Or we may think of it as a hearing aid that enables us to shut out the ambient noise and hear more clearly what God is saying. It is most definitely not meant to be a looking glass in which we admire our own wise faces!

Jesus, the living Word, speaks through the Spirit to my intuitions. The Spirit is the Advocate, the one Jesus promised the Father would send to teach his disciples and remind them of all he had said (John 14:26) and lead them into all truth (John 16:13).

Jesus also speaks in community through others—sometimes the wise mentors who know me (and my proclivities!) and often through those who are different from me. God tunes my inner ear to different tones and accents.

I can know that the voice of God will always direct me to be in line with what Jesus calls us to do—preach the good news to the poor, offer life in all its fullness, announce the coming of the kingdom of God, and make disciples in all nations.

The late E. Stanley Jones, that stalwart Methodist evangelist and missionary, recalled a time when he needed reassurance that God was at work in a hard and broken world. This verse rose out of his Bible reading and spoke to his condition: "Let us be grateful for receiving a kingdom that cannot be shaken" (Hebrews 12:28 RSV).

Reflecting on this Jones wrote, "The kingdom of God gathers up all the loose ends of life and weaves them into total meaning. It is the Cosmic Loom upon which all the little things and big are woven into fabric, into meaning."[2]

I can take up that same refrain. To see the threads that God weaves into the fabric of my life. To trust that he is leading me to be part of that "kingdom that cannot be shaken" in the midst of life's earthquakes.

As I respond to his calling, I may make mistakes. But he does not. And even my mistakes he can weave into his pattern.

The more I listen to him, my true Lord, the more I discover my own voice. The note of his incomparable voice may be heard, through mine.

So I do not let go of the thread.

"This is my Son, whom I love. Listen to him."

I continue to listen. Have I truly heard? And answered?

Now, sooner rather than later, I may have the opportunity to ask that directly.

And I trust to hear that Voice again: "Yes, Leighton, you did hear my voice. Now, welcome."

~17~

SUMMONED
TO ATTENTIVENESS

Give your entire attention to what God is doing right now.

<small>MATTHEW 6:34, THE MESSAGE</small>

Have you seen a burning bush recently? Not a wildfire. A bush on fire but not burning out of control. If you were driving to some appointment and did see one, what would you do? Stop the car? Walk over to see this strange sight? Talk to it? (Not before a nervous look around to see if anyone was watching.)

The story of Moses' calling shows the importance of paying attention. Consider Moses. The son of Jewish parents, adopted by the daughter of Pharaoh, and raised in a palace. He fled Egypt after killing an overseer who was beating a Jewish slave, and he then worked as a shepherd for his father-in-law.

While leading his flock through the desert, he saw a bush on fire (Exodus 3).

"I will go over and see this strange sight—why the bush does not burn up," Moses said to himself.

When he turned aside—*when he paid attention*—the Lord spoke to him.

Moses discovered that the ground where he was standing was sacred. Not the ground of the royal palace of Egypt where he had been raised but the ground out in the hills. There he learned who God was in a new way. God was the great I Am who saw the suffering of his people enslaved in Egypt. Moses learned what his calling was. "I am sending you to Pharaoh," said the Lord, "to bring my people the Israelites out of Egypt."

What if Moses had not turned aside to see? Would the Jews have remained in Egypt, taunted and enslaved? Would God have made a detour around Moses and called someone else? And what would Moses have missed? He would have been an ordinary shepherd for the rest of his life. Not that herding sheep was wrong, but he would have missed his special calling.

What do you and I miss if we don't pay attention?

Consider this: a Washington, DC, newspaper arranged for the world-renowned violinist Joshua Bell to play in a subway station during rush hour. People rushed past, ignoring the music, distracted and in a hurry. A few dropped a dollar or two in his violin case, never realizing how much they'd have to pay to go to one of his concerts. One small boy wanted to stop and listen but his mother pulled him on. Think what they missed!

We are too often distracted people in a distracting world. As technology visionary Linda Stone has said, we pay "continuous partial attention."[1] What do we miss?

Instructions for Living a Life

The poet Mary Oliver offers her "instructions for living a life."

Pay attention
Be astonished
Tell about it.[2]

Good instructions. But so often I don't pay attention. I am not astonished. And at the end of a day I don't have anything to tell about.

When I was writing *The Attentive Life*, my son-in-law asked why I was writing it. "Because I find it so hard really to pay attention," I said. "I need it."[3]

Attentiveness is an ancient, simple, yet difficult discipline. But it is so vital if we are to listen for and discover the voice of our calling, as Moses did when he turned aside to see that burning bush.

The Summoned Life

In *The Road to Character*, David Brooks writes: "A vocation is not a career we choose, but a calling to which we respond. . . . We don't create our lives; we are summoned by life. . . . A person does not choose a vocation. A vocation is a calling."[4]

Brooks has it right. So often our career plans begin with self and end with self. But we know from Scripture that calling begins with God and ends with God.

This is just the opposite of the existentialist philosophy that to live an authentic life means to make of ourselves and our life whatever we want, regardless of what God or anyone else may want. It is also different from the demands for us to conform to some corporate culture.

Creative calling begins not with us but with God the Creator, who calls each of us to be a singular part of his purpose: to form a people for himself. That is the great Story. The impulse to be part of this story comes from God. He finds a way to get our attention. Shows us a need or an opportunity or a danger to avoid. Shapes us and prepares us for his purpose. Through his Spirit, he guides us, liberates us, and accompanies us as we take creative action to carry out his plans.

So it was with the great characters in the Bible. God got Moses' attention with a burning bush. He got the boy Samuel's attention in the middle of the night with a quiet voice calling his name. He got Mary's attention with the vision of an angel. He called Peter through a stranger by the lake who invited Peter to leave his boats and his nets.

An image that reflects this pattern is the Celtic cord. Our personal lives and our vocational lives are woven together as part of God's great pattern. As Paul put it, God works all things together as we are called "according to his purpose" that we may truly reflect "the image of his Son" (Romans 8:28-29).

We see this pattern continually repeated. God gets our attention. Calls us to see what is needed. Then guides us into our own creative ways to carry out his purposes through the gifts he has given us, in the places where he puts us. As we practice using our gifts, we are ourselves also being shaped.

In the novel *Merlin*, Stephen Lawhead's character Merlin says: "The higher a person's call and vision, the more choices are given. This is our work in creation: to decide. And what we decide is woven into the thread of time and being forever. Choose wisely then, but you must choose."[5]

Observe, Reflect, Act

Some years ago I heard of a Catholic leader who formed a significant youth movement in Belgium after World War II. He did so not by telling young people what to do but by teaching them to read the Bible, to pray, and to observe, reflect, and act.

It suggested a process that has helped me to pay attention and that I have often shared with emerging leaders.

Imagine yourself, I ask, as a flight controller guiding airplanes through the sky, gazing at a radar screen, watching the blips moving across in various patterns, and using your brain and training to guide the planes on the right path.

Then I suggest: imagine yourself in a similar process as you seek to discern your calling.

Observe. Look carefully around until you see a "blip" that grabs your attention. It may be a person whose ministry you admire. It may be a need in the community or the world that moves you. It may be an experience that fulfills you and gives you a sense of rightness. Something draws you to say, "I'd like to do that. Try that. Be involved in that."

As John Wesley said, we should "second the motions of the Holy Spirit." So observe what God is doing and where you might fit in.

Early on, Billy Graham and other young and dynamic preachers caught my attention. As I watched and listened I was caught up by the way they moved their hearers. They spoke with energy, vivacity, and conviction. Their personalities and styles were different. Some were a bit eccentric. But their passion was clear. The response was electric.

At the annual Youth for Christ conferences I not only heard them speak from the platform but also saw them late at night, prostrate in prayer, pleading for God's power. "Lord," I prayed, "please use me as you are using them."

They were one of the "blips" on my own radar screen. I began to think: I'd like to preach like that. I think I could. I will try.

Among some old photos, I came across one of a small brick church on the north shore of Lake Erie, not far from my home. There I preached my first sermon. My sermon was overdramatized. It almost makes me blush to think of it. But at the end a young Japanese Canadian girl walked to the front to give her life to Christ, the first of many who would respond across the years. I had a lot to learn about preaching, but my prayers and aspirations began to be answered.

Reflect. Take time to think, to pray about this impression that comes to you. Read about it, especially as you read your Bible. Learn all you can about what you are observing.

Ask questions of people you respect. Be open to affirmations or reservations. Ask a small group of those who know you best to speak into your life and help you get clarity. Most of all pray and pray and pray. And wait for the vision to form.

At that burning bush, when Moses was eighty and two-thirds of the way through his life, he had a dialogue with God that changed his course and the course of the Jewish nation forever.

I have never seen a burning bush, but I have sensed at times an inner burning that has led to my own dialogue with God and to the rekindling and redirecting of my calling.

When the time came for a major change in direction in our ministry, a group of friends who knew me well came to spend a day with me. Their listening was akin to what the Quakers call a "clearness committee." They asked probing questions, listened carefully, raised concerns I hadn't thought of, prayed with Jeanie and me for guidance, and became strong supporters of our new call to identify and develop an emerging generation of leaders.

The insights and wisdom and questions of trusted friends, and most of all of my wife, Jeanie, have been of tremendous value. She has been a part of every major decision and direction both in our family and ministry. On the Myers-Briggs Type Indicator I tend to be motivated by intuition, Jeanie by sensing. My tendency to overthink solutions needs the balance of her practical sense.

Burning bushes and other "signs" in nature can call us to pay attention. But most often my burning bush has been something a person says that brings a fresh idea or opens up an opportunity. There was the seminary president who asked me to lecture on evangelism, resulting in my first book. The TV news anchor who stopped me in a shopping center and suggested that with all the bad news I provide a daily inspirational feature for the evening news, relating the Bible to current events. The head of the Urban League in Seattle who showed me the searing poverty of the inner city and urged me to give a call for action.

But how could I know whether these truly reflect the mind of the Lord?

Prayerful reflecting on these prompts in the light of Scripture has been all-important. Occasionally one particular verse or word lights up my thoughts. More often it is the totality of Scripture, read in light of the words and acts of Jesus, that brings confirmation or causes caution.

With all the good counsel from outside, this reflective process must also be deeply internal. Imagine, I suggest to a younger leader, that you have an inner wisdom circle in which every part of yourself—reason, intuition, emotions—has a voice.

After many years, I had to step aside as chair of the Lausanne Committee because of the pressures of starting our new ministry. It was a painful decision. The fellowship and the vision were precious to me. Some members of the committee were disappointed with me. But my stomach was churning with the stress of trying to carry too much. My body was an integral part of the dialogue. And it was telling me, "time to let go."

On the other hand that call can be affirmed through a deep sense of joy and rightness. In Frederick Buechner's well-known phrase, "The place where God calls you to is the place where your deep gladness and the world's deep hunger meet."[6] And, I would add, where the Spirit's deepest promptings bring a deepening conviction of being in the right place.

Act. Act even in small, beginning ways. Take some creative steps to test whether this gift or calling is truly from God through you. And then your community may affirm (or otherwise) that this is a direction to go.

Jesus described himself as the good shepherd, the one who leads his sheep "to come in and go out," *in* to find life and nourishment, *out* to find "other sheep" and bring them in.

That's what happened with shepherd Moses. At that burning bush he discovered God and his call to action. "Come," said the Lord, "I will send you to Pharaoh to bring my people the Israelites out of Egypt." It was a daunting call. Moses was abashed. "Who am I to do this?" he protested. But God promised both his presence and all the resources he needed, and said, "Go."

And Moses did.

A Fit to Our Calling

Usually, there will be a "fit" to our true calling, a sense of rightness, and fulfillment.

When I asked my son-in-law, a respected ob-gyn, if he had been summoned to his work, he answered, "Absolutely. I was called by joy. The joy I felt the first time I delivered a baby in my training. To be in that room. All the emotion. It was a moment that family would never forget. I felt connected, a horizontal connection to all the people in the room, a vertical connection to the Creator of all life."

I have worked as an evangelist, as a leader, and as a developer of younger leaders. In each of these roles, when I see people connecting with the new and abundant life in Christ and finding for themselves life in all its fullness, it brings me the deepest sense of joy and satisfaction.

A conviction flowing from deep inside says, This is what I am summoned for. If this is not the Spirit bearing witness with my spirit, then I do not know what is. For, as Jesus said, out of the Spirit flows rivers of living water (John 7:38).

But it is more. The summons is not only to something we do but is done to us and in us. Vocation is related to vocal, to voice. It has to do with what we do but also what we are becoming. It is the finding and sounding of our own voice—to know and sing the music of our soul.

Again I think of Moses. We revere him as lawgiver, as leader. He carried out those roles powerfully. But do we also remember

Moses as the one who went to the mountain? Who saw God face-to-face? Whose countenance, after he came down from the mountain, so shined that the people could not look him in the face?

The law came through him, true. But grace and truth came through Jesus Christ. And that's what Paul remembered when he wrote that Moses had to wear a veil to keep the people from gazing at the glory in his face.

What does that have to do with our calling?

All of us, with unveiled faces, seeing the glory of the Lord as through a mirror, are being transformed into the same image from one glory to another; for this comes from the Lord, who is the Spirit (2 Corinthians 3:18).

In all that happens, God is at work in us who are "called according to his purpose . . . to be conformed to the image of his Son" (Romans 8:28-29). In all that we do, our purpose is to reflect the grace and glory of Christ; this too is our calling.

As Gerard Manley Hopkins put it in his poem on Mary, we all, like her, have this *one* work to do: "Let all God's glory through."[7]

So it was with Moses. The end of Moses' wandering journey is fascinating. We have no record of how he died or where he was buried. Why no information on where he was buried or how (except for old age) he died?

Perhaps this mysterious ending for Moses' earthly existence offers a clue to our own calling. Whatever we do, life is always an unfinished symphony. We are never complete in this life. As we follow our present callings *here*, we are being prepared for our final calling *there*, with God.

In Paul's words to his Corinthian friends. "I tell you a mystery: We will not all sleep, but we will all be changed" (1 Corinthians 15:51).

Or as John wrote, "Beloved, we are God's children now, and what we will be has not yet appeared; but we know that when he appears, we shall be like him, because we shall see him as he is" (1 John 3:2 ESV).

Or as Ruth Graham has inscribed on her memorial plaque at the Billy Graham Library: "Construction complete. Thanks for your patience."

∂18∞

THE SOUND OF THAT VOICE

He calls his own sheep by name and leads them out.

JOHN 10:3

*It's as though we can hear not perhaps a
voice itself, but the echo of a voice.*

N. T. WRIGHT

Names matter to God. Over and over in the stories of the Bible names are called: Adam, Abraham, Moses, Samuel, Isaiah, Mary, Peter.

Jesus pictures himself as the good Shepherd who "calls his own sheep by name and leads them out. . . . He goes on ahead of them, and his sheep follow him because they know his voice" (John 10:3-4).

A friend asked a nomadic sheepherder in the Middle East if he had a name for each sheep, and if so how he knew them. He did have names, and also added, "I can tell each one by the shape of its head."

....
187

So when Jesus says he is the shepherd who knows our name, it is because he knows us intimately, the shape of our life, the contours of our heart, and, even more, the person we are created to be.

We might define a Christian as one who, when called by the shepherd, listens and responds. One who hears the call of Christ and pursues that call.

And why should we listen?

We will find full life. As Jesus said of those who follow, "I have come that they may have life, and have it to the full" (John 10:10). If we want full life—listen.

We will find our true selves as he calls us "by name" (John 10:3). As we hear that one "incomparable voice," we begin to find our own voice.

We will find our deepest calling. "I have other sheep that are not of this sheep pen. I must bring them also. They too will listen to my voice, and there will be one flock and one shepherd" (John 10:16). Jesus calls us to join with him in calling others.

The Ones Jesus Called by Name

There are actually only a handful or people recorded who Jesus called specifically by name.

There was Zacchaeus, the little tax collector who perched in a tree, watching as Jesus passed by. "Zacchaeus," he called, "come down immediately. I must stay at your house today."

Martha, Jesus' dear friend and hostess, was so preoccupied with fixing a meal that Jesus gently chided her, "Martha, Martha, you are worried and distracted by many things."

After his friend Lazarus died, Jesus went to his burial place and, convulsed with grief, called, "Lazarus, come out!" And he did.

When he tells his disciples that he is leaving to go to his Father's house, Philip interjects, "Show us the Father." Jesus answers, "Don't you know me, Philip, even after I have been among you such a long time?"

When Mary stands weeping at Jesus' tomb, and, mistaking him for the gardener, asks where his body has been laid, Jesus speaks one word: "Mary!"

Later Saul, the number-one enemy of Jesus and his followers, hears the voice of one he thought was long dead: "Saul, Saul, why do you persecute me?"

I wonder, what would it be like if Jesus called my name?

Would he call me, like Zacchaeus, to stop being a curious spectator, to come down out of my remote tree to share a new life with him? Or, like Martha, to stop being distracted and pay attention to what matters most in my daily life? Or, like Philip, to see the face of God in Jesus and know I can trust him forever?

Would he speak to me, as to Mary, the word of comfort when one I dearly love has died? Or would he surprise me as he did Saul, telling me I had no idea how much he loved me, even in my resistance to his grace?

I am drawn especially to Jesus' singling out of Peter because I learned in those adoption orders that Peter was the name given to me by my birth mother.

When Jesus first encounters Peter, he *calls* him. First by his common name—Simon—and then a new name: "You will be called Cephas" or Peter (John 1:42).

Later, after Peter denies Jesus and is so ashamed that he goes back to work as a fisherman, Jesus *recalls* him. Three times Jesus addresses him by name. "Simon son of John, do you love me?"

(John 21:15-17). And three times he recalls him to his true vocation, "Feed my sheep."

Those words to Peter so beautifully illustrate the voice of our calling.

They tell me that God's call—Jesus' call—to us is not primarily about our life's work, our calling in the sense of the tasks we *do* (though it will include that). It is first of all a call about who we are to *belong to* and who we are to *be*: "You *are* Simon; you *will be* Peter." It is a lifelong call to discover our real names, our truest identities, our deepest belonging.

It speaks of our most authentic and personal vocation: to love Jesus and to feed his sheep—to call and love others as Jesus has called us. It is the strongest affirmation that Jesus calls me when I am starting out with him and keeps on recalling—again and again—to be the person he wants me to be.

In *My Utmost for His Highest*, Oswald Chambers wrote about the time when Jesus tells his disciples that they must become as little children to enter the kingdom. "These words of our Lord are true of our initial conversion, but we have to be continuously converted all the days, continually to turn to God as children."[1]

I have never, as far as I know, heard the voice of God or Jesus, at least not with these ears of mine, or seen him with these eyes. Although I know, or have read about, some who have.

I have not had these experiences.

But I have been listening—with inner ears—to a voice calling. I have a sense of being led. And as sure as I can be that I haven't heard God's voice physically, I am just as certain that I have heard a voice calling.

If the poet Gerard Manley Hopkins is right that "Christ plays in ten thousand places, lovely in limbs, and lovely in eyes not his to the Father through the features of men's faces," then God is calling to us, perhaps, in ten thousand different voices.[2]

How Might This Voice Sound?

If right now the Lord walked up the back steps to where I am sitting on my porch, I wonder, how might his voice sound?

- like the voice of someone I have known and knew I would recognize when I met him
- like a distant hunter's horn in the morning, rousing the deepest longings of my heart
- like calling out from a high cliff and hearing the echo back from a lake below
- like a voice of healing, a balm of quietness, calling a frenzied soul to rest
- like the sound of sheer silence, as it was to Elijah
- like the voice of the beloved in the Song of Songs bounding to me over the hills
- like the whisper of God across my heart
- like the memory of the best dream I ever had
- like the voice of assurance that makes me say, "Now I become myself"
- like the voice of an everlasting love that will not let me go
- like the echo of eternity
- like a voice that queries, "Who do you most deeply want to be?"
- like the exhausted cry of a starving child in Somalia

- like the voice of rushing waters
- like the shaking of some huge trees
- like the crack of a whip in Jesus' scathing words to the Pharisees
- like an unutterable desolation—his cry on the cross
- like a friend who knows me through and through and loves me through it all
- like the voice of a savior calling, "Come to me and find rest for your soul"

A voice that promises, to each of us by name, "Follow me, and I will make you all that I have called you to be."

ACKNOWLEDGMENTS

Since this book is about listening I gladly thank those who have listened to me as I wrote—with encouragement and good guidance. First of all is my beloved Jeanie who knows me and listens to me better than anyone. When I listen to her, I always benefit. When I don't, I usually regret it! I am grateful that my friends at InterVarsity Press, who have published most of my previous books, were willing to listen to what I wanted and to publish a somewhat different book this time. Thanks Cindy Bunch for taking that risk and Ethan McCarthy and Drew Blankman for your editing skills. And to Cindy Kiple whose cover design makes me want to look and listen. My agent and friend Kathy Helmers kept after me for several years, assured me when I was in the doldrums that the story was worth telling, and skillfully rearranged in part the order of my story. Cindy Crosby by phone and email read and reread and made the most valuable suggestions in the writing process. For the friends younger and older who insisted the book was worth writing and promised to read it, thanks. I trust I listened well to all above. As for my recall of years past, I have listened as well as I could to the storehouse of memory and am thankful now still to have good if not perfect remembering!

NOTES

1 The Earliest Voices

[1]Charles Wesley, "Father of Jesus Christ, My Lord," 1742.
[2]Leonard Cohen, "Anthem," *The Future*, Columbia Records, 1992.

2 Discerning One Voice from Another

[1]Gordon T. Smith, *The Voice of Jesus* (Downers Grove, IL: InterVarsity Press, 2003), 24.

3 Choosing to Become a Listener

[1]John O'Donohue, *To Bless the Space Between Us* (New York: Doubleday, 2008), 36.

4 Called to Lead, Led to Preach

[1]John Masefield, *The Everlasting Mercy* (New York: Macmillan, 1913), 78.

5 Crossing New Thresholds

[1]Rainer Maria Rilke, *Letters to a Young Poet*, rev. ed. (1934; repr. New York: W. W. Norton, 1954), 27.
[2]N. T. Wright, *Simply Christian: Why Christianity Makes Sense* (New York: HarperOne, 2006), x.
[3]Penelope Lively, *Dancing Fish and Ammonites: A Memoir* (New York: Penguin, 2013), 147.
[4]Mary Oliver, "Spring," in *Evidence* (Boston: Beacon Press, 2009), 15.

....
195

6 *The Mentor and the Mockingbird*

[1]Mary Oliver, "The Mockingbird," in *A Thousand Mornings* (New York: Penguin, 2011), 31.

[2]Gerard Manley Hopkins, "As Kingfishers Catch Fire," *Poems and Prose* (New York: Penguin Classics, 1985), 51.

[3]James Denney, *The Death of Christ*, (New York: A. C. Armstrong, 1903; Eugene, OR: Wipf and Stock, 2005), viii.

8 *Voices in a Dark Night*

[1]Parker J. Palmer, *Let Your Life Speak: Listening for the Voice of Vocation* (San Francisco: Jossey-Bass, 2000), 70.

[2]Parker Palmer, "Leading from Within," *Learning in Action*, 1994, https://learninginaction.com/PDF/Leading.pdf.

[3]T. S. Eliot, *Four Quartets* (New York: Harcourt, 1943, 1971), 59.

[4]John Polkinghorne, "Quarks and Creation," interview by Krista Tippett, *On Being with Krista Tippett*, March 10, 2005, NPR, https://onbeing.org/programs/john-polkinghorne-quarks-and-creation/.

[5]Thomas Keating, *The Human Condition* (Mahwah, NJ: Paulist Press, 1999), 29.

[6]Keating, *The Human Condition*, 38-39.

9 *Pieces in the Identity Puzzle*

[1]Dante Alighieri, *The Divine Comedy 1: Hell*, trans. Dorothy L. Sayers (London: Clays, 1949; repr. New York: Penguin, 1950), 71.

[2]Helen M. Luke, *Dark Wood to White Rose: Journey and Transformation in Dante's Divine Comedy* (New York: Parabola, 1989).

[3]Thomas Keating, *The Human Condition* (Mahwah, NJ: Paulist Press, 1999), 35.

[4]Christian Wiman, *My Bright Abyss* (New York: Farrar, Straus and Giroux, 2013), 64.

[5]Will L. Thompson, "Softly and Tenderly," 1880.

[6]Richard Rohr, *Everything Belongs* (New York: Crossroad, 2003), 78.

10 *Losing a Son, Restoring a Soul*

[1]Leighton Ford, *The Attentive Life: Discerning God's Presence in All Things* (Downers Grove, IL: InterVarsity Press, 2008), 146-48.

[2]C. S. Lewis, *A Grief Observed* (New York: HarperOne, 1994), 11.

[3]Richard Rohr, *Falling Upward: A Spirituality for the Two Halves of Life* (San Francisco, CA: Jossey-Bass, 2011), 1.

[4]Mary Oliver, "The Summer Day," in *New and Selected Poems*, vol. 1 (Boston: Beacon Press, 1992), 94.

[5]John O'Donohue, *Beauty* (New York: HarperCollins, 2004), 179.

11 A Mantle Falling, a Seed Growing

[1]The source of the quote "The seed is always buried in the dark earth" is unknown.

[2]Amy Carmichael, *His Thoughts Said . . . His Father Said* (1941: repr. Fort Washington, PA: CLC Publications, 2007), 15-16.

12 The Start of a Second Journey

[1]May Sarton, "Now I Become Myself," in *Collected Poems 1930-1993* (New York: W. W. Norton, 1993).

13 A Voice After the Hurricane

[1]The first few pages of this chapter are adapted from Leighton Ford, "After Hugo 3," *Leighton Ford Ministries* (blog), accessed July 9, 2014, www.leighton fordministries.org/2014/07.

14 When We Lose Our Way

[1]David Wagoner, "Lost," in *Traveling Light: Collected and New Poems* (Urbana: University of Illinois Press, 1999), 10.

[2]Philip Yancey, *What's So Amazing About Grace?* (Grand Rapids: Zondervan, 1997), 70.

15 The Voice of Beauty

[1]John O'Donohue, *Beauty: The Invisible Embrace* (New York: HarperCollins, 2004), 13.

[2]George Wade Robinson, "Loved with Everlasting Love," 1890.

[3]This and the next five paragraphs are adapted from Leighton Ford, "Artists of the Soul," *Leighton Ford Ministries* (blog), June 23, 2014, www.leighton fordministries.org/2014/06/23/artists-of-the-soul.

[4]William Stafford, *The Way It Is* (Minneapolis: Graywolf Press, 1998), 42.

[5]Vincent van Gogh, letter to Emil Bernard, June 27, 1888, cited in David Paul Kirkpatrick, "Vincent van Gogh: Jesus Was an Artist Greater Than All Other Artists," *Living in the Metaverse*, March 27, 2013, www .davidpaulkirkpatrick.com/2013/03/27/vincent-van-gogh-jesus-was-an -artist-greater-than-all-other-artists.

16 A Voice Among the Voices

[1]John Polkinghorne, "Quarks and Creation," interview by Krista Tippett, *On Being with Krista Tippett*, March 10, 2005, NPR, https://onbeing.org /programs/john-polkinghorne-quarks-and-creation/.

[2]E. Stanley Jones, *Beginning with Christ: Timeless Wisdom for Complicated Times*, comp. Anne Mathews-Younes (Abingdon, 2018), 227.

17 Summoned to Attentiveness

[1]Linda Stone, "Q & A: Continuous Partial Attention," Linda Stone, accessed May 30, 2019 https://lindastone.net/qa/.

[2]Mary Oliver, "Sometimes," in *Devotions* (New York: Penguin, 2017), 105.

[3]Leighton Ford, *The Attentive Life: Discerning God's Presence in All Things* (Downers Grove, IL: InterVarsity Press, 2014).

[4]David Brooks, *The Road to Character* (New York: Random House, 2015), 24.

[5]Stephen Lawhead, *Merlin* (Westchester, IL: Crossway, 1988), 328.

[6]Frederick Buechner, "Vocation," in *Wishful Thinking* (New York: Harper & Row, 1973), 95.

[7]Gerard Manley Hopkins, "The Blessed Virgin compared to the Air we Breathe," *Poems and Prose* (New York: Penguin Classics, 1985), 55.

18 The Sound of That Voice

[1]Oswald Chambers, "Continuous Conversion: December 28," in *My Utmost for His Highest* (Uhrichville, OH: Barbour, 1935).

[2]Gerard Manley Hopkins, "As Kingfishers Catch Fire," *Poems and Prose* (New York: Penguin Classics, 1985), 51.